Field Work

ALSO BY ANDREW FORBES

FICTION

The Diapause
McCurdle's Arm
Lands and Forests
What You Need

NONFICTION

The Only Way Is the Steady Way: Essays on Baseball, Ichiro, and How We Watch the Game
The Utility of Boredom: Baseball Essays

Praise for Field Work: On Baseball and Making a Living

"What a mind Andrew Forbes has, and how lucky we are that he's given over so much of it to thinking about baseball — sifting through its bottomless history for bits of gold, diving with gusto down its quirkiest rabbit holes. He's a five-tool talent, and with *Field Work* he stakes his claim as baseball's most indispensable folklorist. This collection of essays is the purest expression yet of his love for the game and the men who played it for a living."—Devin Gordon, author of *So Many Ways to Lose*

"Canada's resident baseball philosopher has done it again, offering a typically charming collection of quirky essays tying America's pastime to universal facets of life, love, and—as the title suggests—work. To read this Andrew Forbes book is to lose oneself in a world of baseball mysticism grounded in the decidedly un-mystic world of hard (and sometimes not-so-hard) labour. Savour it in pieces or gobble it down all at once; either way, you'll be glad you did."—Jason Turbow, author of *They Bled Blue*

Praise for previous baseball writing by Andrew Forbes

"Transcendent prose."—*Shelf Awareness*

"You do this for long enough, and you begin to crave originality like a desert wanderer craves cool clear water. Andrew Forbes's essays are cool and clear and may well slake the thirst of any thinking baseball fan."—Rob Neyer, author of *Power Ball: Anatomy of a Modern Baseball Game*

"This essay collection is a rainy-day read of a memoir from a Canadian writer and baseball traditionalist who comprehends the game at an elite observational level, yet writes about it accessibly. He believes watching or listening to a ball game will help soothe the anxieties brought on by the coronavirus. The same could be said for his relaxing, lucid essays."—*Globe and Mail*

"Taking his cues from Susan Sarandon's character in *Bull Durham*, who worships at 'the Church of Baseball,' secular humanist Forbes finds something close to religion in everything from Jose Bautista's bat flip to the Billy Ripken error card."—*Quill & Quire*

"A splendid meditation on life and the game… Forbes' essays are as consumable as a large tub of popcorn."—FanSided

"In all of these essays, Forbes's writing is almost invisibly stunning, clear, with romantic flourishes equal to his subject matter. But what he's really able to articulate is how a love of baseball is really about a love of, or at least an acceptance of, the fact that losing is part of the game."—*National Post*

"Andrew Forbes opens the dome on inside baseball, bringing to the often stats-rigid game the same warm, curious insight that marks his underrated short fiction."—*Canadian Notes & Queries*

"A thoughtful consideration of the sport, creatively told through scorecards, baseball cards, and open letters to Ichiro Suzuki, the Japanese-born baseball star whose charismatic personality and achievements in the game have made him a fan favorite for two decades."—*Ralph Lauren Mag*

Field Work

ON BASEBALL AND MAKING A LIVING

ANDREW FORBES

Assembly Press
Prince Edward County, Ontario

Library and Archives Canada Cataloguing in Publication

Title: Field work : on baseball and making a living / Andrew Forbes.
Names: Forbes, Andrew, 1976- author
Identifiers: Canadiana (print) 20250135213 | Canadiana (ebook) 20250135221 | ISBN 9781998336159 (softcover) | ISBN 9781998336166 (EPUB)
Subjects: LCSH: Baseball. | LCSH: Labor. | CSH: Canadian essays (English)—21st century. | LCGFT: Essays.
Classification: LCC PS8611.O7213 O53 2025 | DDC C814/.6—dc23

Published by Assembly Press | assemblypress.ca
Cover and interior designed by Greg Tabor
Edited by Andrew Faulkner

Printed and bound in Canada on uncoated paper made from 100% recycled content in line with our commitment to ethical business practices and sustainability.

For CC
and Kevin
and Mom

"Baseball to me was more work than play."

— TY COBB

"This is a job. I do this to make a living."

— ANTHONY RENDON

TABLE OF CONTENTS

RECORD OF EMPLOYMENT

On The Sporting News's *player index cards*

From the 1880s until the advent of electronic sources like baseball-reference.com, whether you were a casual fan, a devoted partisan of a particular team, or a baseball journalist, if you really wanted to know what was happening in baseball, you turned to a few trusted print sources. Daily papers devoted considerable column inches to covering the game, but it was the weeklies that went deep. The *New York Clipper* had broad distribution and featured copious baseball coverage. *Sporting Life* was published in Philadelphia and was, according to its front-page motto, "Devoted to Base Ball, Trap Shooting and General Sports," with regular contributions from Henry Chadwick, baseball journalist and inventor of the box score. But *The Sporting News* was the longest lived of these publications. Dubbed the "Bible of Baseball," it was founded by a Canadian and, for most of its print run, based in St. Louis.

Alfred Henry Spink was born in Quebec City in 1854, and while still a boy, he moved with his family to Chicago. Al's older brother William relocated to St. Louis, where he served as sports editor for the *Globe-Democrat*; William convinced his kid brother to move to the Gateway City. Al became a sports journalist too, and he and Billy became active and important organizers in the city's sporting life. In 1886, after stints with the St. Louis *Post*, the *Globe-Democrat*, the *Missouri Republican*, and the St. Louis *Chronicle*, Al Spink decided to go it alone.

The first issue of his new weekly, *The Sporting News*, was published on March 17, 1886. It promised coverage of "The Wheel," "The Gun," "The Stage," "The Ring," and "The Turf," but it leaned toward baseball. The publication's success was both the result of and a contributor to St. Louis's reputation as the best baseball town in the world.

Sometime in 1886, the editors of *The Sporting News* undertook a feat of record-keeping astonishing in its thoroughness and of incalculable value to later baseball scholarship: they started the Player Contract Cards Collection, a vast store of index cards containing biographical and contract information for every single professional ballplayer. The three-by-five-inch cards were typewritten, with occasional remarks or annotations in pen. The collection was maintained until 1991, when the information was computerized, and holds the details of 172,000 players and about 10,000 umpires and team executives. The cards were donated to the Society for American Baseball Research in 2013 and painstakingly digitized, and they're now searchable online.

A card, in its practised shorthand, a mix of typewriter ink and dashed handwritten annotation, might read:

Name	**Position**	**Bats**	**Throws**
Pruett, Hubert S.	-P-	R	L
Born-Place Higginsville, Ky.	**Date** 9/1/1900		**Married**
Address 7449 W. Florissant Florissant, Missouri		**Height** 5'10½	**Weight** 165
Teams Played With Missouri Univ. 1920-Tulsa 1921-St. Louis A.Lg. 1922			

Pruett's card sits alongside those documenting the full array of baseball talent, from incandescent stars like Cobb ("Born-Place: Narrows, Bank County, Ga."), Ruth ("George (Babe) Herman"), and Robinson ("football–basketball"), to lesser-known members of the fraternity like Arlie Latham ("Employed at Polo Grounds and Yankee Stadium from 1932 until last fatal illness"), and Harry Simpson ("Goody"; "Married Miss Johnnie M. Cooper, August 15, 46").

As a whole, the collection is a roll call of men who made a living playing the game of baseball. On an individual level, a card is a record of employment, proof that each of these players—all 180,000 of them—suited up to play professional baseball, whether for one game ("Graham, Archibald Wright... New York NL 1905–"), or 3,652 ("Rose, Peter Edward... Placed on Ineligible List by order of Commissioner 8/23/89–").

The cards—tactile, fragile, messy—speak to a pre-digital world, and a game that shared those characteristics. The records they hold, available still for scholars or the merely curious, preserve in ink on paper the employment status of thousands of men across ten and a half decades. In aggregate, they constitute a massive trove of information about a group of individuals spanning economic and social lines who shared a profession, a fraternity of workers who donned uniforms and equipment to jog out onto baseball diamonds, their jobsites landscapes of dirt and grass.

THE NEIGHBOURHOOD PLAY

On the spirit versus the letter, and being against precision

A few years back, on a balmy Tuesday evening in early summer, my son, Theo, suited up in his Peterborough Tigers uniform for his first Eastern Ontario Baseball Association U12 game of the season against the Uxbridge Grizzlies. He stood tense in the right-handed batter's box and took a couple pitches. "Working the count," he calls it; "not swinging," I call it. The next pitch came inside and—maybe, possibly—lightly brushed the front of his jersey, between the navy blue and orange *Tigers* lettering and his belt.

"Batter, take your base," said the umpire, pointing with his right arm down the line to first.

Theo, who must not have felt the ball and doing his best, bless him, to live by the credo of honesty, said, "But it didn't hit me."

The umpire continued to point. Calls began to rise from Theo's coaches and teammates to heed the ump's directive. After a brief interval of confusion, he laid down his bat and jogged up the line.

On the drive home, Theo said, "I swear it didn't get me."

"Maybe," I said, "but if the ump's trying to give you something for free, take it."

Without really meaning to, I had given my kid a lesson in the rudiments of moral relativism. At least as it pertains to games, or at least as it pertains to baseball. He might have interpreted the message a bit more broadly than that, but I think this is one of the values of sport, the understanding that while rules are rules, some rules supersede others. You have to prioritize.

According to rule 5.05(b)(2) of the Ontario Baseball Association's official rule book, the batter "becomes a runner and is entitled to first base" when they are "touched by a pitched ball" that is not in the strike zone, provided the batter attempted to "avoid being touched by the ball." It further clarifies that the batter "shall not be considered touched by a pitched ball if the ball only touches any jewelry being worn by a player," suggesting via elision that a player whose regular uniform is brushed by a pitched ball may jog to first base.

Rule 8.02 further states that "any umpire's decision which involves judgment, such as, but not limited to, whether a batted ball is fair or foul, whether a pitch is a strike or a ball, or whether a runner is safe or out, *is final*" (emphasis mine). "No player," it continues, "manager, coach or substitute shall object to any such judgment decisions."

This is a mighty rule that trumps so many others. Whether or not Theo was "touched by a pitched ball" outside the strike zone, if the umpire said he was, Blue's decision was final.

Baseball is a game of decisions. Swing or take? Run or hold? Take the sure out at first or try to nail the lead runner? Yank this pitcher or give him one more out? And in cases where one disagrees with an umpire's call, which rule applies to the particular situation and what are the potential consequences of skirting it? When I disagree with the umpire's call, is it worth arguing the decision?

More than how to field a grounder, hit a breaking ball, or execute a hook slide, I think this is the real take-away from months of hot and buggy practices, back-to-back doubleheaders, and chaotic tournament weekends: Developing that barometer. Learning to navigate moments of ambiguity, to know when to protest, turning your palms heavenward in petition, and when to shut up, drop your bat, and head up the line to first.

★★★

In the wake of the economic upheaval brought on by the Covid-19 pandemic, a buzzy new term crept into the public lexicon: quiet quitting. It applies to workers' actions when, for spite, private protest, or the maintenance of mental health, they resolve to do only what is strictly necessary or contractually required to hold on to their jobs. The spiritual cousin of work-to-rule, it asserts that a human being is more than a worker. Quiet quitting affirms belief in work–life balance and that extra hustle results in an insufficient payoff.

Whether working from home and Zooming into meetings or donning an apron and showing up in person, young workers understood the value of their labour, and that their employers, by and large, failed to recognize that value. Underpaid, overworked, and frequently put at risk—especially those in what had been considered unskilled jobs, whose presence proved vital to the continued existence of economic activity during lockdowns—workers recognized a rare reversal of power. Food service professionals, store clerks, and delivery people became heroes.

Quiet quitting is a passive response to the gulf between valorizing language and the actual treatment of young workers.

Wages stagnated even as the cost of living shot up. Job security was revealed to be a fairy tale, benefits rare, and advancement generally blocked by aging workers who refused to retire. Quiet quitting emerged as the latest step in the dance between authorities and plebeians, an assertion of real agency, a wresting of control.

Many workers went further, and the result was dubbed the Great Resignation. Take this job and shove it, thousands said, because there's a better one available to me. And for a time, there was: national coffee chains were temporarily closing locations that didn't have enough employees to operate.

This meant that if you wanted a job, especially a service sector job, you could find one. Unemployment numbers, which shot up in early 2020 and remained there for months, dropped as people returned to work. There was upward pressure on wages. Many office workers who'd set up remote workstations in their homes and could now wear sweatpants to meetings balked when asked to return to a physical office; instead, many went looking for more flexible employers. All of this nudged some power back toward labourers and granted them a modicum of control over their working lives.

This wasn't a trend isolated to North America. In China, the tang ping movement (from the Chinese meaning "lying flat") gained traction, inspiring many to adopt a lifestyle devoid of ambition, performing only those tasks deemed absolutely necessary. If action led to longer work hours for diminishing rewards, scaling back one's involvement in a predatory system through inactivity seemed like a sane response.

As the world is currently arranged, power settles where the money gathers, i.e., in the hands of the overclass. And so wages soon flattened in the West, inflation went ballistic, rents hiked, and any advantages working people had gained were subsumed by macrotrends in the zombified afterlife of capitalist enterprise. Employers compensated for fleeing and "underperforming" workers through downsizing and automation.

The overlords, the owners, the employers: they want it both ways. They would have you do what you're contractually obligated to do, and more—whatever it takes to help the enterprise grow, to enrich them and their peers, while you gain not a smidge more than that to which you're legally entitled.

It's a question of the spirit versus the letter. Your employer wants you to go above and beyond, to embody the spirit of your role, to carry a flag for the organization, even as they want to guarantee you only what's strictly spelled out in their contracts and pesky legislation. Conversely, workers decide that if they're only receiving what's in writing then they'll only give what's in writing. It comes down to a misalignment of expectations and desires. In setting their borders, the sides have staked out starkly divergent territories.

No workplace is immune. All of this, alongside unfortunate advancements in high-definition video technology, explains the adoption of instant replay in baseball.

Modern instant replay is so granular it's nearly atomic, and it's changed how the game is played. It used to be that a fielder could toe the base a smidge before catching the ball, or a titch after throwing it, and still be credited with retiring the lead runner in a double play. Now, instead of solely relying on instinct, umpires get New York on the phone, where faceless forensic specialists at the Replay Operations Center pore over the tape to make sure the timing was perfect, then call back with their judgment. Same goes for runners sliding into bases. In the past, if you beat the ball to the bag, you were safe, but with the clarity of replay, a runner who's safe but who subsequently loses contact with the base for a fraction of a second can be called out. Fielders know this, so once they stick their tag, they hold it there until the play is called dead.

★★★

Doug Harvey umpired 4,673 National League games over thirty-one seasons, from 1962 to 1992. He was a hardened adjudicator so respected that players called him, quite sincerely, "God." Harvey was even-handed, deliberate, and unflappable. Did Doug Harvey blow some calls? Yeah, he did, because Doug Harvey was a human being. But his misses didn't dent his credibility one bit. That's the way things sometimes shake out, and if a bad call went against you when Harvey was behind the plate, you knew that sooner or later you'd get one back.

I'm trying to imagine Doug Harvey donning the headset to ask New York to scrutinize a play, and so to scrutinize his judgment. In a procedural sense, I think Harvey's nickname was apt and should effectively be used to refer to all umps, at least between the lines, and between the first pitch and last out. The umpire's authority within that delineated patch of earth should be absolute. In bowing to a manager's demand and calling for footage to be reviewed, an umpire forfeits his authority to technology and to a room full of anonymized people who can't be booed or heckled by forty thousand sun-drunk partisans.

The effective heckling of umpires is an artistic discipline that requires logic, erudition, and the quick humour of a stand-up comedian, and when performed well, it adds a wonderful dimension to the experience of attending a ballgame. There's nothing like shouting a zinger ("Hey, Umpy, you're missing a great game!") to vent your frustration and amuse your fellow fans, uniting you all in the reassuring embrace of perceived victimhood. But if the object of your derision is several time zones away? Or built by Sony? The exercise is robbed of its verve.

In the case of close plays, it seems to me that truth is less important than maintaining a clear hierarchy of governance alongside jurisdictional transparency. The field ought to belong to the umpires—marshals of order—with the crew chief atop them all. Fallibility is part of the deal; if perfection is the goal, then once we replace all umps with cameras, I can't see why we wouldn't just swap the players for robots. Then we can all sit back and place our bets.

Like so many of us, today's umps are being closely monitored for inefficiencies, while their technologically superior replacements wait in the wings for the flip of a switch that will allow them to assume complete control. Robots won't miss that third strike on the outside corner, but they also won't appreciate the beauty and importance of their task.

I resent instant replay because it's so precise. I believe baseball is a far more approximate game than Bill James and his revolutionary guard would have us believe. It's better to let imprecise legend reign. How far did Mickey Mantle hit that ball in Washington? Roughly a mile. Did the shortstop brush the toe of his shoe across second base at the very moment he received the flip from the second baseman? Close enough! Was the would-be thief still in contact with the bag when the defender tagged him a second time? Pretty damn approximately!

Did that ball hit Theo? More or less.

★★★

Rules are important. Honesty is the best policy. Generally. Baseball is a game, and games are amusements that humans are alone in concocting—placing ourselves in artificial peril in order to experience the thrill of escaping it. In a certain regard, games are akin to a collective hallucination. They're played within a set of invented strictures. Baseball is the cousin of a verbal contract, an IOU written in disappearing ink. The stakes are essentially fictitious.

I'm not counselling you to completely flout all rules, or to bang on a trash can like the 2017 Astros. Though I will admit to finding romance in the lore of the fabled espionage operation that may have helped Bobby Thomson hit the Shot Heard 'Round the World in 1951. Is it time alone that makes the Astros hateable and Thomson's homer romantic?

Even where the stakes are real, some pushing back at directives is necessary, as is doing only and exactly what you can get away with. (These beliefs may explain why I'm essentially unemployable.) Ours is an imprecise world, morally speaking, and you, me, and everyone we know are going to spend our brief spans operating in that ambiguity. So, I reasoned, Theo might as well get used to it in youth baseball.

I could feel Theo over my right shoulder, maybe looking at me in the rear-view mirror as we drove home from his game. Was I really telling him to cheat?

Theo had advanced as far as third and was stranded there, so whether or not he was actually hit by that pitch did not reflect in the final score. Like most of our moral quandaries, this one was swallowed by the vast scale of the universe, one inconsequential action lost amid the shuffle of atoms and the velocity of our spinning.

They're going to ask more of you than they're willing to give, I might have said. They'll perform bag checks after every shift, maybe random drug tests. They'll want to monitor your keystrokes. They'll want you to work late, to shorten your break, to answer emails at 9:00 p.m. So if that inside pitch merely whizzes past your billowing jersey without so much as grazing the grey polyester, but the ump sees it otherwise? That's a gift, kid, one you should accept.

Batter, take your base.

WORKINGMAN'S BLUES

On jobs held while hanging on

Ted Wilks worked in a power plant. Nate Fisher was a banker.

Sidearmer Jim Bunning was the Phillies' representative to the Players Association, a stockbroker, and an insurance salesman during his playing days. Once retired from the game, he ran for office, serving in the Kentucky Senate, the US House of Representatives, and the US Senate.

Richie Hebner dug graves in the offseason.

Reliever Blake McFarland's baseball career topped out at Triple A, so he pivoted to art, sculpting animals from recycled tires, metal, wood, and a variety of other materials. He's still working as an artist today and is available for commissions.

Doc Bushong was a dentist and a catcher for the St. Louis Browns.

Shags Horan played professional soccer.

★★★

For every Shohei Ohtani or Aaron Judge—megasuperstars on their way to billionaire status—there are thousands of players who've had to supplement sparse baseball earnings with offseason jobs, or part-time work, or who returned to the workforce once the dream dried up. They've slung booze across sticky counters, they've put spades into earth. They've sold cars and shirts and insurance policies. They're the rank and file, and they make up the vast majority of those who've suited up to play professional baseball. For most of the game's long history, ballplayers have been paid to throw and hit. But historically most haven't made enough, so they've had to get creative to patch together a living.

★★★

When his baseball career stalled during World War II, Danny Gardella moved in and out of many jobs, finding work as "an elevator operator and house detective at the New Yorker Hotel," according to SABR biographer Charlie Weatherby. As "a railroad yard freight handler... a shipyard stevedore, and... a trainer and masseuse at Al Roon's Gym."

With many established players serving overseas, a lot of guys got a shot at the bigs they might not otherwise have gotten. Gardella had a punctured eardrum that earned him a 4-F classification from the military, so he wound up with the Giants instead of shipping off to the front. After his baseball career was well and truly over, Gardella worked as a singer, an athletic trainer at a hotel in the Catskills, operated a drill press for the Otis Elevator Company, opened a restaurant that didn't last, and worked in a Western Electric warehouse.

Moe Berg was a spy. While touring Japan with Babe Ruth's American League All-Stars in 1934 he shot home movie footage he later showed to the Office of Strategic Services, figuring it might assist them in identifying bombing targets. Though the film would prove to be of little value to the military, Berg later formally joined the OSS.

Jophery Brown became a stuntman.

Jason Conti became a chef.

Carl Furillo opened a deli.

Johnny Berardino was an actor with bit roles in *North By Northwest*, *Them!* and a bunch of TV dusters before landing the role of Dr. Steve Hardy on *General Hospital*, a gig he'd keep for thirty-three years.

Pete Karpuk was a journeyman utility guy who bounced around the minors when he wasn't playing Canadian football for the Ottawa Rough Riders, Hamilton Tiger-Cats, or Montreal Alouettes.

Mickey Mantle mined zinc and lead. Three Finger Brown dug for coal.

★★★

A surprising number of players trod the boards, either in the offseason or once retired. Cap Anson, John McGraw, Turkey Mike Donlin, Christy Mathewson, and Rube Marquard all spent time on Vaudeville stages. So did Rube Waddell, who also wrestled alligators.

Waite Hoyt appeared frequently on Vaudeville too, when he wasn't busy with his mortuary business or selling his paintings. He also spent twenty-four seasons in the broadcast booth for the Reds.

★★★

Even after the rise of the Major League Baseball Players Association in 1966, players who'd yet to make the majors remained unorganized, with no collective agreement, and most had to find second or third jobs to get by. A 2023 agreement saw minor-league players organize for the first time, creating the MiLBPA and reaching an accord with Major League Baseball on wage increases as well as improved housing and facility standards.

Prior to the agreement, a player in rookie ball (the first level a player entered after being drafted) was paid $400 a week during the season, and nothing for the rest of the year, which works out to roughly $10,000 per annum. The minor leaguers' first collective deal set salaries at $19,800 for an entry-level player, with levels increasing as he moved up the organizational chain, topping out at $35,800 for a Triple A player, with each player also receiving $250 a month in the offseason to continue his year-round training.

★★★

Arlie Pond earned his medical degree from the University of Vermont in 1895 before heading to Baltimore for postgraduate studies at Johns Hopkins. While at Vermont he'd excelled as a varsity pitcher, so Ned Hanlon, manager of the Orioles, convinced Pond to spend his summers playing ball. At spring training in 1895, infielder John McGraw contracted typhoid, and it was Pond who recognized the severity of Muggsy's case and brought him to a hospital in Atlanta. McGraw stayed while the team went north, remaining hospitalized until June, and he didn't rejoin the team until August. Pond played four years for the Orioles, winning thirty-five games, before leaving the game and becoming an Army surgeon.

Pond's one-time teammate, shortstop Hughie Jennings, began studying law at Cornell in 1899. He also coached the Cornell baseball team in lieu of paying tuition. Though he didn't finish all his classes, he passed the bar exam, and for decades thereafter, while managing the Tigers and Giants, he maintained a legal practice in the offseason.

Steve Trout pitched for the Cubs, White Sox, Yankees, and Mariners, then retired and wrote books, including the illustrated children's title *Loosey-Goosey Baseball*, which he self-published in 2015.

The players on the Czech Republic's 2023 World Baseball Classic team all had day jobs. The roster included a firefighter, a salesman, a financial analyst, a high school geography teacher, a real estate agent, and a media coordinator who worked for a Czech Baseball Extraliga team—for which he also played. The Czech manager was a neurologist. In a qualifier against Samurai Japan at the Tokyo Dome, in front of over 41,000 fans, Ondrej Satoria, an electrician, struck out Shohei Ohtani with a 79 mph fastball and two changeups.

A young Stan Musial, a few years from stardom, was newly married with a baby on the way when he began earning offseason money as a clerk in his father-in-law's grocery store.

Teenage righty Alta Weiss, said to have a lively fastball and a dipping curve, spent two summers barnstorming around Ohio, leading a team called the Weiss All-Stars. People turned out in good numbers to see the "Girl Wonder" take the mound. The money she earned put her through school. In 1914, she was the only woman to earn a degree from the Starling Medical Academy. She practised medicine until her retirement in the late 1940s.

Livings cobbled together, baseball dreams deferred, or savings banked in service of an off-field dream—there's no textbook approach to the relationship between working and playing.

Labourers with bat and glove, labourers with pick, pencil, industrial press, stethoscope. Are the figures on the diamond playing or working? The language can be muddled, contradictory. Spend enough time with the question and the distinctions fade, grow obscure. Those figures are best described, maybe, as simply living.

SHUCKS

On origins, chance occurrences, and a young lefty who walked into a ballpark

In 1920, Hubert Shelby Pruett walked up to Sportsman's Park in St. Louis and was offered a contract to play big-league baseball.

It was like that then. You could be a pretty good hitter or pitcher, or a fast runner, and someone would see you and figure you just might be good enough to play professionally. A bird dog would fill your ear with promises of big-league glory in the hopes that, should another roving scout happen along with another halfway decent offer, their ornate version of the future would be enough to ensure your loyalty. The scout would recommend you to whichever organization he was affiliated with, formally or otherwise. With luck, a contract would be proffered, the scout would get his cut, and you'd be on your way.

Hubert Pruett—often "Hub," and to others "Shucks," because that was said to be the saltiest word in his vocabulary—was a promising pitcher. As an undergraduate playing at the University of Missouri, he was spotted by Cardinals scout Charley Barrett, who told the young hurler that if he ever wanted to play pro ball, he should head up to St. Louis and they'd see what they could do for him. So one June day Shucks made his way to St. Louis and presented himself at the Cardinals' offices at Sportsman's Park.

But the Cards were on the road. Finding no one at the team's office at 3623 Dodier Street, or at least no one who'd heard of Hubert Pruett, he must have wandered to the Browns' suite, located around the corner at 2911 North Grand Boulevard.

It's worth considering just how rare this particular circumstance is—two big-league teams sharing one stadium—though it's not unprecedented. In 1914 and '15, both the National and American League Boston clubs played at Fenway Park. The Yankees moved into the Giants' Polo Grounds and played there from 1913 until 1923 when they opened their own park in the Bronx. In Philadelphia, the Phillies moved into the Athletics' Shibe Park in 1938 and the teams shared the facility until the A's left for Kansas City in 1954. In the '70s, the Yanks shacked up with the Mets at Shea Stadium while Yankee Stadium was undergoing renovations. And then there's St. Louis, where the Cardinals moved in with their crosstown brethren in 1920. But that's it; otherwise, major-league teams have enjoyed the sole everyday use of their own baseball fields.

Bob Quinn, the Browns' business manager, was kicking around Sportsman's Park that June day. He greeted Hub, listened to his story, and asked if Hub wanted to play big-league ball for the Cardinals, or if he just wanted to play big-league ball. Hub said it didn't matter to him, so Quinn offered to let Pruett work out for Browns manager Jimmy Burke.

Burke was impressed, so the Browns offered Shucks a contract.

★★★

In 1879, desperate to retain their best players at reasonable rates, National League owners instituted a rule that allowed them to "reserve" five players on their roster for the following season. In time, the number of reserved players grew, until every standard player contract included the clause, which effectively allowed an organization to retain players indefinitely—and to set their salary, since a player's only recourse, if he didn't like the terms, was to sit out. Doing so would result in a salary of $0 and would prevent the player from taking his services elsewhere.

This is the contract that Pruett—and anyone else who played big-league baseball for nearly a century—would have been given the opportunity to sign.

★★★

It's tempting to think that the most interesting aspect of Hub's story is the happenstance of being offered a contract to play for the Browns only as a result of the Cardinals being on the road and the two clubs sharing a ballpark. Another day, or a different schedule, and Shucks quite possibly would have found himself in the National League, where he wouldn't have had the chance to do what eventually made him notable.

There's a version of this tale that frames Hub as an ambitious young ballplayer who'd do anything to get to the big leagues, so he signs with the Browns because he doesn't care which cap he's wearing, only that he gets his shot to show what he can do. That's interesting, too.

For my money, though, we haven't even gotten to the most fascinating part.

PLACES OF BUSINESS

On the origins of professionalism, the mutability of American cities, and the many ballparks of St. Louis

In 1858, Brooklyn's governing council challenged New York—really, the island of Manhattan—to a three-game series to determine which city was tops in the increasingly popular game of base ball (or base, or base-ball, or baseball).

The game was still in its amateur era, a popular recreation enjoyed by adults in their leisure time. Clubs were organized and the participants, especially in New York and Brooklyn, began to codify the rules of a game that looked very similar to what is played today. But nobody was paid to play.

Not that there wasn't money floating around the game: the gamblers had long taken notice of the contests and their variable outcomes, which satisfied all the conditions necessary for wagering.

For the Brooklyn–New York challenge series, players were selected for each team from the many amateur clubs in the area, and the matches were set to be played at Elysian Fields in Hoboken, New Jersey—a peaceful green idyll a short ferry ride across the Hudson River that served as home to many of the game's pioneering early clubs, including the famed Knickerbockers. As the contests neared, however, the organizers, taking the temperature of public discourse, opted to resituate the series in a venue capable of accommodating greater crowds. The site they chose was a horse track in Queens called the Fashion Race Course, very near the spot the Mets' Citi Field now occupies. Its grandstand had a capacity of ten thousand, with standing room for many thousands more around the playing surface.

The first game of the series has gone down in history as the first time that spectators paid to see a baseball game. Admission was ten cents, plus twenty cents more to stow a one-horse conveyance—then as now, you might find a deal on tickets, but the parking will kill you. The stated reason for the charge wasn't profit or to pay the players, but to cover the costs of repairing the grounds after the ballplayers were through tearing it up. Any leftover funds were to be donated to orphans and widows. There are no official attendance figures available to us today, but it's commonly believed that anywhere from four to ten thousand people showed up.

Four years later, William Cammeyer, owner of a plot of land in Williamsburg, Brooklyn, was looking for a way to use the property year-round. The site contained a winter skating pond for which Cammeyer charged admission. After surveying the sporting scene, Cammeyer opted to convert the space into baseball grounds. His innovation was to enclose the field: he had a grandstand built that would seat 1,500, and as with the Fashion Race Course, many more could be accommodated about the field's margins.

The horseshoe-shaped grandstand looked out over the diamond and an enormous field. Cammeyer named it the Union Base Ball and Cricket Grounds, and its outer reaches contained a strange feature: in deep centre field stood a flag-topped pagoda, a remnant from the skating pond, conspicuous and in play.

As with the one-off horse racing track arrangement, paying the players wasn't part of Cammeyer's business model. Instead, admission revenue would stand in place of charging the tenant ballclubs rent. The Union Grounds was the first baseball facility to be built specifically for spectators—fans who, author and historian Thomas Gilbert suggests, differ from mere watchers (or gamblers or family members) in that they possess a "voluntary emotional commitment" to the proceedings, generally based on civic or local pride—and feature amenities for their comfort and enjoyment, as well as for the convenience of the players.

The facility opened with an exhibition game on May 15, 1862, with an estimated three thousand people on hand. Three clubs quickly took up regular residence at Cammeyer's grounds, and many other teams would make use of the park in the twenty years it operated.

Once the Union Grounds were built, says Gilbert, "you can't stop the ball rolling toward professionalism." But it's worth noting that the first to be paid—the *first* baseball professional—wasn't a player the public was paying to see, but Cammeyer, the facility's owner.

Competition shortly ensued: the Capitoline Grounds opened just down the road two years later, and it too proved successful. A ballpark building boom followed, and it soon reached every corner of the United States.

These new buildings, dedicated to containing the game of baseball and the crowds that would gather to watch it, were amusement palaces for the nineteenth century's emergent American leisure class to take in an entertainment spectacle while reinforcing notions of ownership and enclosure, both physical and economic. For many of us, stadiums play host to magical events, but they also don't exist without the cold realities of class division reinforced by capital. Ballparks, like the cities in which they are built, are born into history, not outside of it. They're platted within the linear, social, temporal confines of human endeavour, both bearing the impressions of, and imprinting their marks on, the American landscape.

★★★

When, in 1920, Hub Pruett walked into the offices at Sportsman's Park, he was entering just one of the many ballparks to have been built in St. Louis.

Had he travelled south on Grand Avenue, he'd have found himself amid a cluster of old baseball addresses loosely grouped along the east–west Clark Avenue corridor. Where Gratiot Street met South Compton Avenue, the Red Stockings of the National Association of Professional Base Ball Players held games during the 1875 season on six acres of flat turf that spectators could take in from a wooden grandstand. On May 4 of that year, the Red Stockings hosted the first professional iteration of the Brown Stockings, who had entered the National Association in 1875. The two tangled at the Reds' grounds in the first openly professional baseball game in the city's history. The Browns prevailed 15–9. Losers on the field and outduelled for the city's affections by the Browns, the Reds dropped out of the National Association after the 1875 season, reverting to amateur status (as they'd remain for the rest of their existence) but continuing to occupy the park. The Red Stockings' grounds were torn down sometime around 1898, and the site is now the central operations yard for the St. Louis MetroBus system.

While it stood, occasional lessees of the facility included the St. Louis Black Stockings, one of the first all-Black clubs in the nation. Their manager, Henry Bridgewater, pushed for the creation of a professional Negro League, a dream that wouldn't be realized until Chicago's Rube Foster steered the organization of the Negro National League decades later.

The Black Stockings were enormously successful. They toured the country to take on quality amateur teams, drawing large crowds, including once luring an estimated four thousand to the Red Stockings' yard in 1883. But they had no field of their own and were forced to rely on white teams' willingness to rent their facilities. This would generally prove to be the case for Black baseball for the duration of its existence, from the late nineteenth century until the Negro American League bowed out in 1962.

Just up the road from the Red Stockings' grounds, the Brown Stockings established their base. The Brownies had entered the new National League in 1876 but resigned from the organization following the 1877 campaign in the fallout of a game-fixing scandal. Iterations of the club wandered through the amateur and semi-professional barnstorming desert until 1882, when German-born saloon owner Chris von der Ahe purchased the club and changed their fortunes—and his own. The beer garden he owned in this early version of Sportsman's Park (literally *in*; suds were served in a pavilion that sat in play in right field) swelled with patrons. Rebuffed in his efforts to have the Brown Stockings join the National League, he helped establish the American Association—the "beer and whiskey league"—the venues of which featured cheaper admission, abundant liquor and, unlike the NL, games on Sundays.

In 1893, the Browns' owner would open a new park—unimaginatively named New Sportsman's Park—just a few blocks northwest of their original grounds. Von der Ahe poured resources into the new grounds, and streetcars brought fans almost directly to its front gate, but the old boss was bleeding money, which was exacerbated when the new park caught fire—twice. In the end he was forced out and ownership was transferred to Frank De Haas Robison, who made over New Sportsman's Park into League Park.

The team eventually earned a berth in the NL, and, before the turn of the century, changed their name to the Cardinals. Shortly after, Milwaukee's American League club relocated to St. Louis, taking up residence in the *original* Sportsman's Park at Grand and Dodier, and adopting the Browns name.

When the Federal League declared itself a third major league in 1914, the St. Louis Terriers began to play in Handlan's Park, directly west of the campus of St. Louis University. That park sat on land owned by Alexander H. Handlan, whose company manufactured railroad hardware. A grandstand, pavilion, and bleachers accommodated fifteen thousand spectators, and the lot was squeezed on its northern and southern edges by housing. After the Federal League imploded a couple of years later, the space became the SLU athletic field and hosted the teams of two nearby high schools, and thus became commonly known as High School Field.

The St. Louis Giants were an independent Black squad founded in 1906 that led an itinerant existence, playing on several different diamonds, including Handlan's, and touring the Midwest to match up against a number of Black teams dotting the area. Many of those teams, including the Giants, would become members of Rube Foster's Negro National League in 1920, though in that first year all of them would only play as tenants of white teams in their home cities.

Giants manager Charlie Mills eventually found partners in St. Louis's white business community to help finance the construction of a proper ballpark for his squad to call home, but the site he chose was in the north end of the city, far from the majority of St. Louis's Black citizens' homes, and the financial burden of building the park forced Mills to relinquish his NNL franchise.

In 1922, the Giants' spot in the NNL was taken by the St. Louis Stars, who staged games at Handlan's until their new home was ready at South Compton and Laclede. With Stars Park, the St. Louisans became one of the lone professional Black baseball teams with a facility built expressly for them to call home. Stars owner Dick Kent called it Dick Kent's Ballyard, an immodest act unless you consider that his park was the first fully African American–owned baseball stadium in the country. Viewed in those terms, the gesture seems appropriate.

Stars Park's wooden grandstand, pavilion, and bleachers combined to seat at least ten thousand. As the plaque now located on the spot attests, Hall of Famers Cool Papa Bell, Mule Suttles, and Willie Wells all patrolled Stars Park's grounds, and the Stars were NNL champions in 1928 and 1930.

This is what was on offer for St. Louis baseball fanatics with open afternoons and streetcar fare in 1922: up on the north side, Rogers Hornsby (.401, 42 HR, 152 RBI) playing second base for the Cardinals; George Sisler (.420, 105 RBI, 51 steals) at first and Ken Williams (.332, 39 HR) in left for the Browns; and farther south, the Stars' outfield of Sam Bennett, Charlie Blackwell, and Doc Dudley, with the rookie Cool Papa Bell, then a pitcher.

The Stars occupied their park until the middle of the 1931 season when the NNL—by then without Foster, who'd been institutionalized in 1926 and died in 1930—succumbed to the Depression and ceased operations. The Stars were declared champions of the circuit's final campaign. In the years that followed, the field's grandstand and field fell into disuse and disrepair.

Happily, the field hosts baseball again today. It sits within the campus of the historically black Harris-Stowe State University. Once again dubbed Stars Park, the HSSU Hornets' field is trim but relatively spartan, with chain-link fencing throughout and a quartet of stand-alone aluminum bleachers flanking home plate. I visited once in the spring, though rain prevented a game from being played. Instead, umbrella in hand, I took in the historic plot where those legends roamed. The grass was green, though patchy in places, and a rough path was worn from the home bench to the batter's cut-out.

Across Compton Avenue, on the same block once occupied by the Federal League park, sits the home of the St. Louis University Billikens baseball team. It's lavish compared to the Hornets' field, and includes artificial turf, a permanent outfield wall, and a concrete grandstand for about five hundred fans. Three-tenths of a mile separate the two facilities—along with a few million dollars.

★★★

In 1920, auto dealer Sam Breadon bought up shares in the Cardinals and, en route to becoming the majority owner, he quickly determined that New Sportsman's Park (a.k.a. League Park, Robison Field, and Cardinal Field) was no longer viable. He negotiated with Browns owner Phil Ball to lease Sportsman's Park—the facility originally built by Chris von der Ahe for the Cardinals, who'd then been known as the Browns.

From the onset of this cohabitation arrangement, the Browns found themselves on the bad end of the deal, collecting lease payments of predetermined value from the Cardinals while remaining solely responsible for the park's upkeep and any required improvements. The Cardinals directed much of their revenue into the development of their farm system, while a succession of Browns owners sunk good money after bad to keep the ballpark in game-day trim.

The Cardinals, under new owner August Anheuser Busch Jr.—"Gussie" was also chairman of the brewing giant—assumed sole ownership of the dilapidated stadium before the 1954 season. Busch poured money into the park, hoping to undo years of neglect, shoring up elements the Browns couldn't afford to address. But the city of St. Louis was changing, roiled by forces both economic and political, and Busch would soon be looking for a new home for his redbirds.

★★★

Nominally, the reason cited for the old Sportsman's Park's obsolescence was a lack of parking, as more fans started driving in from the suburbs rather than taking trolleys. It was also located in an area that many of its would-be customers were being told was unsafe, as Black St. Louisans were moving into housing vacated by white families who'd left the neighbourhood for the suburbs, many in response to school desegregation. The suburbs, accessible through improved roads and transit systems, beckoned middle-class white families in search of more racially homogenous housing, upheld through zoning laws and the unavailability of federal housing loans to Black families.

In 1964, ground was broken on a parcel of land adjacent to I-64 and I-44, in the heart of downtown St. Louis. The property had been made available through the underhanded and generally racist and classist process of urban renewal, a practice fuelled by the belief that there were better—which is to say more profitable—uses to be made of land containing the homes and businesses of minorities. Chinatown was razed, and warehouses, flophouses, and hotels were demolished to make room for the new multi-purpose stadium, with surface parking and easy egress. The new arena was nearly indistinguishable from other ring-style stadiums of its era, often derogatorily referred to as "cookie-cutters," built in Washington, Atlanta, San Diego, Cincinnati, Pittsburgh, Philadelphia, and elsewhere. The sole distinguishing feature of the new Busch Stadium (officially Civic Center Busch Memorial Stadium)—the thing that helped you identify it if you were watching on TV—was its crown of ninety-six mini-arches, each an echo of Eero Saarinen's Gateway Arch, which loomed less than half a mile from home plate.

In a sign of the dramatic changes sweeping the city, the last streetcar in St. Louis came to a halt on May 21, 1966. The last game at Sportsman's Park happened two weeks earlier, on May 8. There were less than eighteen thousand people in attendance to watch the Giants double up the Cards 10–5, capping ninety-one years of professional baseball at Grand and Dodier. After the game, home plate was carried by helicopter to the new stadium. On the evening of Thursday, May 12, forty-six thousand were on hand to watch the Cardinals inaugurate their new digs with a 4–3 win over Atlanta.

Sportsman's Park was torn down and Gussie donated the land to the Herbert Hoover Boys Club (now the Boys and Girls Club), which built a facility on the site that includes a ball field for the young residents of the still predominantly Black neighbourhood.

Just to the south of the ballpark sat the Carter Carburetor plant, which lasted nearly two decades beyond the stadium's demolishing. Sprawling to ten acres in size at its operational peak, the plant made crucial engine components for customers like Chevrolet, Oldsmobile, and Packard. It also produced the contaminants polychlorinated biphenyl and trichloroethylene, and the plant itself contained considerable amounts of asbestos. Once the plant closed in 1984, the lot—just across narrow Dodier Street from the Boys and Girls Club—was fenced off and listed as a Superfund site, a place so contaminated that it was earmarked for rehabilitation by the US Environmental Protection Agency. Cleanup did not begin for nearly thirty years and wasn't completed until 2020. You needn't have extraordinary access to the halls of power to surmise that if the parcel was located in a more "desirable" part of town—if the kids playing ball across the street had been white—it wouldn't have taken thirty years to rid the site of industrial contaminants.

Meanwhile, the new state-of-the-art stadium hosted baseball, the NFL's Cardinals (who'd also played at Sportsman's after moving from Chicago in 1959), soccer, concerts, and other events. It hosted World Series–winning Cardinals teams in 1966 and 1985. It witnessed the careers of Bob Gibson, Lou Brock, Ted Simmons, Ozzie Smith, and manager Whitey Herzog. It was the backdrop for Mark McGwire's 1998 home-run blitz, and it was where he hit number sixty-two on September 8, and number seventy, the last of his record-setting season, on September 27.

By the end of the century, public favour had turned against cookie-cutter ballparks, and though Busch had more charm than most thanks to its arches and natural grass, its days were numbered. The Anheuser-Busch Corporation, which had taken over ownership of the team after Gussie Busch died in 1989, used the tried-and-true owner's gambit of threatening to leave town—in this case for Madison, Illinois, just across the Mississippi River—in order to get someone else to pay to replace the multi-purpose ring with a baseball-only park built right next door.

The third Busch Stadium opened in 2006, shortly after its predecessor fell to the wrecking ball. It features red brick, open social areas, and architectural flourishes—including iron arches meant to reference both classic ballparks and its immediate surroundings. It has lovely views of downtown St. Louis and the Gateway Arch. It was designed in the vogue of classically inspired new ballparks such as Baltimore's Oriole Park, Denver's Coors Field, and Jacobs Field in Cleveland. The Cardinals, wasting no time, doused their new home in champagne at the end of their first season there, beating the Tigers in five games for their first championship in twenty-four years.

On Paul Goldschmidt's 2020 Topps Stadium Club card, the burly Cardinals first baseman rounds third in a trot at Busch Stadium III, likely having just hit one of the thirty-four round-trippers he clubbed in 2019. Bright sunshine illuminates the field and a dazzlingly blue sky is accessorized with a skein of fluffy white cloud, artfully framed by the Gateway Arch's solid silver bracket. It looks like an image from a tourism brochure. It's pretty near perfect.

Not quite visible in the photo, but within its frame all the same, is a site at Clark and Broadway, possibly near where Goldschmidt's shot landed. That's where there used to be a building, erected and owned by Bernard M. Lynch to confine enslaved people, both those to be sold and "fugitive slaves" brought in after their bids for freedom. Lynch also began a fugitive slave capture business, further profiting from the violent denial of others' freedoms.

When the Civil War broke out, Missouri was a slave-holding state, though it behaved more or less neutrally and St. Louis remained in Union hands. Lynch fled to the South, where he was swept beneath the rug of history, never to be heard from again.

Just off-camera on Goldschmidt's card, about three blocks from the wall in left-centre at Broadway and Market, stands the old courthouse. There, in 1846, the enslaved man Dred Scott and his wife, Harriet, sued for their freedom. The case eventually made its way to the Supreme Court, which ruled in 1857 that African Americans and their descendants were not citizens of the United States, but rather property, and as such were not granted the rights and privileges outlined in the US Constitution.

Spiritual oases to many, ballparks are not exempt from the vicissitudes of history. They weren't when William Cammeyer opened his Union Grounds in Brooklyn, nor when Hub Pruett strode into the shared accommodations at Dodier and Grand, nor when St. Louis's white residents fled the area around Sportsman's Park for the suburbs. And they aren't now, as current owners eye public funds to finance the construction of new ballparks and adjacent real estate developments. Baseball stadiums rest amid and within history, subject to its tides. And you, me, and every ballplayer we've ever cheered for are by definition implicated, no matter how fervently we may wish to cleave our play from the work of the world, in all its complexity, pain, and reward.

CROOKEDNESS AND ITS PENALTIES

On Hal Chase, the 1919 White Sox, sportsbook commercials, and extracurricular activities in pursuit of supplemental income

George Sisler was inducted into Cooperstown's hallowed Hall of Fame in 1939, a member of the institution's fourth class. The men before him are rare idols, a pantheon of immortals that includes Ty Cobb, Christy Mathewson, Babe Ruth, Tris Speaker, Cy Young, and Pete Alexander. Sisler's handsome bronze likeness sits atop a somewhat stilted inscription that lauds his offensive accomplishments and labels him "one of best two fielding first basemen in history of game."

Hal Chase was the other, and he likely holds the number-one spot, at least in the minds of his peers and the baseball establishment—the owners, writers, and attendant personalities who occupied the game's upper echelons when Sisler's plaque was cast.

In his *Historical Baseball Abstract*, writer, historian, and statistician Bill James puts it succinctly: "No other player in baseball history was so richly praised for his defensive skill—no one." So why, scant paragraphs later, when discussing Chase's value and whether he was the sort of player to serve as a team's foundation, does James write, "No matter what his skills, I would not want Hal Chase around, period"—what was Hal Chase's crime?

★★★

For the bulk of the game's history, the system has been rigged imposingly against players, leaving them with three choices: accept it, fight for change, or resort to subterfuge to secure a baseball-adjacent revenue stream. Time and again, Hal Chase chose the latter.

Born in Los Gatos, California, in 1883, Harold Homer Chase was the first player to become a star for the team that would come to be called the Yankees. He played ball at Santa Clara College in 1902 before moving to the Pacific Coast League. Most sources report that the Los Angeles Angels were his first pro team, though his yellowed *Sporting News* player contract card includes a curious entry. Between "Santa Clara College" and "1903-Los Angeles," the card lists "1902-Victoria."

It seems that Chase and a buddy, Elmer Emerson, who pitched at Stanford, trekked north in the summer of 1902 to picturesque Victoria, BC, where Emerson had family, to play for a nominally amateur club. Chase, at least, was paid under the table—seventy-five dollars a month to start, and later ninety. He didn't bother to adopt an alias even though getting paid to play put his amateur status—and his ability to play the following season at Santa Clara—at risk.

Chase doesn't appear to have suffered repercussions for the escapade. At the end of the summer, he returned to Santa Clara College and resumed his amateur career. One game saw him play against St. Vincent's College (now Loyola Marymount University) in Los Angeles, with Angels owner and manager James Morley umpiring. Morley, impressed by what he'd seen, approached Chase.

Of course, the Angels in question were not the American League Angels (familiar today for names like Carew, Trout, and

Ohtani), but rather the PCL Angels, a completely separate entity. The Pacific Coast League (established in 1902) is a minor circuit with teams throughout the western US; in Chase's day, it spread from Seattle to Southern California. As the majors ventured no further west than St. Louis, and as the quality of play in the PCL was quite high, the league drew interest from an enormous area and long functioned effectively as a third major league.

Morley signed Chase to play for the Angels, and Chase, who later bragged that he hadn't attended a single class at Santa Clara, dropped out of school to pursue professional ball. In 1904, Chase was drafted by New York of the American League—then known as the Highlanders—and Morley objected to the process by which his first baseman was being pilfered. The draft was then a process agreed to by all signatory leagues to the National Agreement (the 1903 covenant which governed the leagues' relations to one another, and established the groundwork for the entity we know as MLB)—including the Pacific Coast League—in which teams in higher leagues might "draft" talent from lower leagues by paying agreed-upon fees. The Highlanders paid their fee and considered Chase theirs. But Chase's slow reporting to spring training suggested that Morley was in no hurry to give up his man.

It's unclear how Chase felt about all this, with his soon-to-be-former PCL boss's actions potentially denying him the $2,000 salary New York had agreed to pay him. Chase had become a pawn in an ongoing war between the majors and the minors. In time, Morley lost the support of other PCL owners, who likely feared punitive repercussions and damage to their business model of selling talent to the eastern clubs. Morley withdrew his objection; Chase was a New York Highlander.

★★★

About the amateur era of baseball, author Thomas W. Gilbert writes of the positive (or perhaps not wholly negative) influence of wagering on the sport: "Gamblers promoted interclub play, helped spread baseball beyond New York, and pushed it toward greater organization and transparency." While it's a stretch to say that professional baseball wouldn't exist without betting, it's safe to state that betting has been present as long as the game has been played.

To wit: a match in 1865 between the Mutuals of New York and the Eckfords of Brooklyn was shown to have been "heaved" by three members of the Mutuals after they'd been offered one hundred dollars by a gambler. In 1877, four members of the Louisville Grays of the National League were expelled for conspiring to throw games—probably enough games to have influenced the final standings, in which the Kentuckians finished seven games behind Boston.

These high-profile cases represent the tip of an unfathomably large iceberg. When Nick Carraway asks Jay Gatsby how it was that underworld figure Meyer Wolfsheim happened to fix the 1919 World Series, Gatsby replies, "He just saw the opportunity."

Baseball has always been generous with such opportunities.

★★★

Hal Chase spent over eight seasons in New York, during which he established himself as a good hitter, a great glove man, and a difficult personality. He disparaged teammates and bellyached about the Highlanders' choice of manager. When he felt he wasn't being paid enough, he threatened to jump to an outlaw league where the money was better. He talked his way into the manager's job, then steered the club into a slide in the standings from second to sixth. When first baseman Frank Chance took the reins, Chase showed displeasure sufficient to get himself traded to the White Sox. The rumours that he was crooked, bribing teammates to cook games, and taking and making bets persisted.

★★★

The Federal League began life in 1913, a six-team independent minor league bankrolled by a group of businessmen who, when their ad hoc outfit didn't completely fail in its first season, began to dream audaciously. By 1914 the FL had grown to eight teams, relocated one club (from Covington, Kentucky, to Kansas City), and added teams in Buffalo and Brooklyn. They set their sights on achieving status as a third major league by going head to head with the established loops in Chicago, Brooklyn, Pittsburgh, and St. Louis.

The Federal owners then enticed a number of established players. These players signed with their new clubs knowing full well that to latch onto a team in an "outlaw" league like the FL was to earn a spot on the National Agreement's blacklist. The FL was costing its backers a lot of money, primarily because in order to convince good ballplayers to jump, especially those not contemplating retirement, the new teams had to offer lucrative multi-year contracts. In January 1915, out of desperation, the upstart circuit filed a lawsuit against the established leagues, asserting that their actions violated the Sherman Antitrust Act of 1890, a federal statute aimed at stamping out anticompetitive behaviour—to prevent "restraint of trade or commerce among the several States."

The presiding judge, Kenesaw Mountain Landis, sat on his decision. And sat. The 1915 season began. Still Judge Landis deliberated. By midseason, it began to dawn on several of the Fed owners that their enterprise was doomed financially. The AL and NL owners, meanwhile, understood the very real possibility that Landis would decide in favour of the FL, making them open to dealing with the problem by other means.

A peace agreement was proposed, and among its provisions was that blacklisted Federal players would be allowed to return to American and National League clubs.

The date etched into the Federal League's tombstone is December 22, 1915—the day the peace agreement was signed and the case sitting with Landis was formally dropped. But the FL's Baltimore Terrapins pursued a new lawsuit, and a jury ruled that the established leagues had violated antitrust laws. The judge awarded the Baltimore group $254,000.

The established leagues appealed. Their argument was that baseball did not constitute interstate commerce. In December of 1920, the Court of Appeals agreed. "A game of baseball," wrote Chief Justice Constantine J. Smyth, "is local in its beginning and in its end."

"The players," he continued, "travel from place to place... but they are not the game."

The Baltimoreans next brought the matter to the Supreme Court, which rendered its decision on May 29, 1922—almost seven years after the last Federal League game had been played—upholding the opinion of the Court of Appeals. Wrote Justice Oliver Wendell Holmes, ballgames "are purely state affairs." Baseball, they'd concluded, is not commerce.

The case, known simply as *Federal Baseball*, established Major League Baseball's exemption from antitrust statutes, a status which remains in place.

Hal Chase was among those who'd jumped, moving from the White Sox to Buffalo's FL team in the middle of the 1914 season. Chicago objected. When the dispute made its way into the courtroom, the judge summed up the situation succinctly by calling organized baseball "a species of quasi-peonage unlawfully controlling and interfering with the personal freedom of the men employed." Chase stayed in Buffalo.

When the Fed folded, Chase was kicked loose. Though he was no longer formally blacklisted, Hal had made so many enemies that no American League team would touch him. The National League was another story. The Cincinnati Reds were interested in Chase's services and he became a regular for them in 1916, playing around the diamond as needed and leading the NL with a .339 average. He was the Reds' everyday first sacker in 1917 and enjoyed another fine campaign, though the team treaded water under the managerial stewardship of none other than Christy Mathewson.

If there's a human being with a reputation diametrically opposite to that of Hal Chase, it's Christy "Matty" Mathewson. "The Christian Gentleman," they called him, because he refused to play on Sundays. Universally beloved, Matty had pitched the last of his 635 games for John McGraw's New York Giants in 1916. Slowed by injury and age, Mathewson expressed a desire to manage, so McGraw finagled a trade to Cincinnati where the aged hurler would assume the top post. Nice guys finish last, they say, and that was true for Matty and the Reds in '16. He improved the team to fourth in '17, and third the year after that.

In 1918, the oil-and-water combination of Chase and Mathewson proved immiscible when the skipper suspended the player for throwing games and reported Chase to the National League for offenses against Section 40 of the league constitution, Crookedness and Its Penalties. The statute reads: "Any person who shall be proven guilty of offering, agreeing, conspiring or attempting to cause any game of ball to result otherwise than on its merits under the Playing Rules, shall be forever disqualified by the President of the League from acting as umpire, manager, player or in any other capacity in any game of ball participated in by a League club." It appeared likely that Chase's proclivities had caught up with him and would force him from the game.

But by the time Chase's case could be heard by baseball's National Commission, Mathewson was overseas, serving his country in the army's chemical warfare division in France. With his primary accuser absent, National League president John Heydler reluctantly let Chase off the hook.

★★★

An aside, if you'll permit it.

I'm nearing fifty, and I find the pull of Springsteenian long looks back and Polaroid-tinted nostalgia difficult to resist. Change and distance equal time, and my experience is that as more and more time piles up behind me, the harder it gets to avoid spending quiet moments gazing at everything in the distance. Life is a sitcom and the past is a bunch of your favourite episodes all queued up.

Baseball fandom is particularly susceptible to long looks back. It's a sport with a deep history, a penchant for self-aggrandizing memorialization, and an army of hacks writing endless tomes to its long-dead heroes. (I do not exclude myself from this economy of reminiscence.) The internet is chockablock with niche content devoted to singing the praises of the Deadball Era, the postwar golden age, the seventies, the eighties, the nineties, and the early aughts. And I'm here for all of it. Chubby, mullet-crowned, mustachioed first basemen driving neon yellow Camaro Z28s, smoking Marlboros, chugging Miller Lite, and hitting dingers? Yes, please. Depression-era journeymen with torn and dirty uniforms, missing teeth? Okay! Another photo of Mickey Mantle, Whitey Ford, Billy Martin, and Bob Grimm palling around, sipping Cokes, fishing in their undershirts? How do I subscribe?

I love those earlier iterations of the game, but I'm not too blind to recognize that we're in the midst of a new golden era, populated by some of the greatest players ever to take the field—Ohtani, Acuña Jr., Betts, Cole, etc.—and I further understand that some of my issues with the manner in which the game is being marketed nowadays have everything to do with my age. I'm not the target demo. Which is fair, since I'm hooked regardless.

But with that said, the single greatest threat to my continuing enjoyment of baseball and all other professional sports is the inescapable flood of commercials for legal online sports betting.

I don't bet. And I don't care if you do, if you do so responsibly. It's your money. But I can't help but reflect on all those players who were swallowed up by the very activity. The monied doyens of baseball waged morality campaigns, distancing the game from undesirable elements by periodically culling players caught augmenting their salaries by leveraging one of their few advantages: they played a game people paid to see, and these players' efforts (or lack thereof) determined the winners and losers.

If I were a cynic, I'd say that all this—the terrible commercials, the chumminess of the relationship between Major League Baseball and the gaming industry, the additional billions being raked in by billionaires on the backs of both players and fans plugging wagers into apps while watching at home—lays bare the fact that the early guardians of the game only found gambling repugnant because they weren't getting enough of the take. Now that they have assumed some measure of control of the whole lousy apparatus, they're happy to have baseball and betting mentioned in the same breath.

For a century and a half, the odds on a ballgame were whispered, rumoured, shared in confidence. Baseball's rulers were zealous anti-gambling crusaders, guarding against its incursion into the game with the fervour of religion. If players were spotted too close to the contagion, their careers were set alight.

Then, in 2018, the Supreme Court kicked the regulation of sports gambling to the states, which one by one began to legalize the practice and collect taxes off the money exchanged. To Major League Baseball, as with all other sports leagues, the practice suddenly looked less like a disreputable vice, and more like a torrent of revenue that might be rerouted into owners' pockets. Now, if you tune into a regional sports network to watch your favourite team, the odds flash regularly across the screen, and commercial breaks feature a steady diet of ads for online sportsbooks, reminding you to reach into your pocket, pull out your phone, thumb open an app, and place a bet.

★★★

In 1919, John McGraw, having long ago transitioned from player to player-manager to manager, needed a first baseman for his Giants. Chase, unchastised and available, was his man.

Meanwhile, Mathewson, recovered from influenza and exposure to mustard gas that occurred while in France, returned stateside but found himself jobless. Reds owner Garry Herrmann, unsure when Matty would return, had replaced him with Pat Moran. Mathewson turned to his old friend McGraw, who brought him aboard as a coach. So did Matty and Hal meet again.

Chase played well enough, until he didn't, and by September he was watching from the bench. A bum wrist, he said. There were also suggestions that he'd been paying off teammates. Whatever the truth, the real item of note in Chase's 1919 season concerns conversations with an old acquaintance from his first stint in New York, Arnold Rothstein. Nicknamed "The Big Bankroll," Rothstein was the model for the character Meyer Wolfsheim in Fitzgerald's *The Great Gatsby*, and like that unfortunate caricature, the real Rothstein was always looking for some action. Chase had a tip for him: the World Series was approaching, featuring the White Sox and the Reds. Certain Chicago players might be persuaded to influence the outcome of the Series, went the word.

Rothstein apparently liked what he heard and began to work the angles. The fixing plot became a poorly kept secret. When the Reds beat the heavily favoured Sox and the malfeasance was uncovered, Chase was indicted for being a middleman. Prosecutors failed to establish a link to Rothstein, so no charges were brought against him and he never faced court. Though also charged, none of the Chicago players were convicted either, but that didn't stop newly appointed commissioner Kenesaw

Mountain Landis from expelling—for life—Eddie Cicotte, Chick Gandil, Happy Felsch, Joe Jackson, Fred McMullin, Swede Risberg, Buck Weaver, and Lefty Williams. Common belief has long held that the players, led by Gandil, went in for the scheme because they felt to a man that they'd been undervalued and insufficiently paid by White Sox owner Charles Comiskey.

There might be no event in baseball history more studied than the 1919 World Series and its fallout. Society for American Baseball Research author Bill Lamb sums up recent scholarship on the matter: "salary data recently made available establish that the 1919 Chicago White Sox had the second highest player payroll in the major leagues, with stalwarts like second baseman Eddie Collins, catcher Ray Schalk, third baseman Buck Weaver, and pitcher Cicotte being at or near the top of the pay scale for their positions."

So there goes that theory, though we shouldn't discount the depression in earning power represented by the reserve clause and owners' eagerness to yield it like a cudgel. Salaries had also dipped across baseball in the wake of the Federal League's collapse, and again in 1918 when both the NL and AL played shortened seasons in deference to the nation's efforts in World War I.

The infamous eight might not have been underpaid by the standards of their field, but they evidently still felt the existence of a sizeable gap between what they got and what they believed they were worth. Baseball owners, including Comiskey, were figures out of Gilded Age editorial cartoons: monocled and overfed, heads wreathed in cigar smoke, lording over their fiefdoms and expecting their subjects to show due deference.

There's no shortage of blame on all sides in the affair, but it might be worth considering who was sanctioned and who was allowed to exercise agency. When weighing culpability, the scale doesn't start in a position of perfect balance.

★★★

"Refused to report for 1920," reads *The Sporting News* index about Harold Chase. "Later developments proved he was mixed up in throwing games of World's Series of 1919—barred from all Coast league parks."

He was never formally expelled, but Chase could no longer get a job in any league that adhered to the National Agreement, whether major or minor. He instead spent the bulk of the 1920s as an itinerant, traipsing the literal desert and playing outlaw ball in several Arizona towns. He even secured roster spots for a few of the banned-for-life White Sox. He moved on to Texas and then California. He prospected for gold. He drifted.

His player index card, after noting that he'd briefly been proprietor of an "auto laundry" in Tucson, then concludes, in fainter ink and slightly askew: "Died from kidney ailment & heart trouble at Colusa Memorial hospital, Colusa, Cal., May 18/47."

Like Pete Rose decades later, Chase would cop to being a betting man in sporadic interviews but would remain adamant that he never bet on his own team. He claimed to have had nothing to do with Rothstein or the 1919 World Series. Despite his efforts to clear his name, there was a trail of evidence and ample testimony to tie him to all of it: bribing teammates, almost certainly throwing games himself, and arranging large-scale conspiracies involving dozens of people and tens of thousands of dollars. But his protests prevented him from publicly recording the impetus for all this activity, leaving us to guess whether his actions were spurred by addiction, a sense of injustice, revenge for maltreatment, or the mundane and unquiet ghost of greed.

In 2024, the minimum salary for a Major League Baseball player stood at $740,000. The average player earned in excess of $4 million. It might be that the game's stewards believe that such hefty paycheques alleviate any temptation toward betting on games that a given player might reasonably influence. If so, the stewards hold a different understanding of human motivation than I do.

As for Chase, whether you condone or condemn his actions, you have to hand it to him: his greatest con might have come years after he stopped playing. For as careful as baseball has been to distance itself from games of chance, as pure an image as it strives to uphold, the doyens inadvertently let Prince Hal slip into the sacred corridors of the Hall of Fame. His likeness was never cast in bronze, but he's there, an elision, a suggestion, the cipher-like presence right there on Sisler's plaque, unnamed. For a shark like Chase, it's the ultimate tribute: he's credited, but never directly implicated.

LAYERS

On Chicago, Picasso, and the strata of history

There's no place like Chicago. My wife, Christie, and I have visited on a few occasions, and each time we've made a point of going to the Art Institute. The last time we were there, we happened on an exhibition of Picasso's drawings, and in it we encountered *The Frugal Meal* (1904). It's a stark etching of a seated couple, almost Giacometti-like in their emaciation, harshly lit, the hatted man looking off to the viewer's left, the woman delicately resting her chin on her hand with her head cocked to the right and her eyes cast toward the ground at some scrap of memory left discarded there. Before them on a table is a bottle of wine, two glasses, an empty plate, a small crust of bread, and another object, small, perhaps a hunk of cheese. The subjects' limbs and extremities are rendered almost comically long and lean, their faces gaunt, bones jutting, as was Picasso's style in his Blue Period.

The etching is part of a collection of prints dubbed La Suite des Saltimbanques (The Acrobats Suite), depicting Parisienne circus performers that a young Picasso executed in hope of improving his financial circumstances. *The Frugal Meal* is haunting, its subjects so abject in their need, that it presages the coming horrors of the epoch that Picasso had only just entered, which would see empires fall, global wars waged, and systems of government finding new ways to control and exploit populations.

Chicago's Art Institute is housed in two wings: the original limestone-faced 1893 Beaux-Arts edifice, with its lion-flanked entrance, arches, and columns, and the much more recent Modern Wing, which appends the original building via a bridging structure that straddles a tangle of railroad tracks. At one point Christie and I found ourselves standing in the latter, in a windowed atrium that contained only a single painting—Francis Bacon's horrifying *Figure with Meat* (1954)—and a complete wall of windows overlooking the northwest quadrant of Millennium Park. From those windows, the train tracks are invisible. Just out of view, the rail lines duck under a massive deck that supports the park.

In their open spaces, cities can't help but reveal their layers. Our north-facing view revealed the green of the park overtop the railyard and its chrome bean-shaped *Cloud Gate* sculpture (Anish Kapoor, 2006), and the globular latticing and folded/crenelated form of Frank Gehry's Jay Pritzker Pavilion bandshell (2004). Beyond are the modern forty-one-storey limestone and aluminum facade of One Prudential Plaza (1955), and the granite verticality of the Aon Center (originally the Standard Oil Building), which, at eighty-three floors, was for a few months in 1973 the tallest building in Chicago. It's a vista marked by sere public-facing displays of twentieth-century wealth, corporate muscle, urban planning, and civic beautification. In their silence, though, the skyline's features issue implicit self-rebukes for the failure of the American city to provide for all its residents while upholding the credo of modernity: dismantle and start again. Bulldoze. Raze. Build atop. Go higher.

And in that idyllic, money-encircled quadrant, bordered by Michigan Avenue to the west, East Randolph Street to the north, and South Columbus Drive to the east, on ground previously used as an open-air midden, there once stood a ballpark. From 1878 until 1884, Chicago's National League ballclub—called the White Stockings then, and now the Cubs—played in a couple iterations of what was known as Lakefront Park, a wooden structure with a short right-field line that was eventually augmented with a screen. Under Cap Anson—an unrepentant racist who became the game's most vocal proponent of a colour line—and featuring King Kelly, George Gore, and Larry Corcoran, the White Stockings won a string of pennants at Lakefront. In 1884, on that same spot, Providence pitcher Charles "Old Hoss" Radbourn beat Anson's squad in late September for his fifty-sixth victory of the season, en route to a never-to-be-beaten record of sixty wins.

After the 1884 season the city assumed the land on which the ballpark stood, absorbing it into the railyards, which remained the block's prominent feature until the completion of Millennium Park in 2004. The White Stockings moved to West Side Park, a facility built in part from lumber salvaged from Lakefront. The ballclub christened their new home with a pennant in 1885.

It's to Christie's credit that she can suffer this so often, knowing that wherever we travel, at least in North America, no matter the cultural riches on offer—stunning architecture, renowned collections of art, musical and theatrical performances, bars and restaurants and taverns—I can be counted on to say, "You know, there used to be a ballpark here."

The American League's Chicago White Sox began life playing at South Side Park, with a wooden grandstand built by Charles

Comiskey for his new team at the dawn of the twenty-first century. A decade later Comiskey moved his club a few blocks north, into the new steel and concrete stadium that would eventually bear his name. The grounds abandoned by the Sox would become home to Black baseball pioneer Rube Foster's Chicago American Giants.

The White Sox played in the Zachary Taylor Davis–designed ballpark until 1990. In 1991, when they moved next door into their new stadium (which has worn a series of corporate monikers in the decades since its opening), old Comiskey Park was demolished to make way for the new building's parking lot. But its ghost remains, most visibly in the form of the old home plate and batter's boxes, recreated on the asphalt.

As Christie and I toured the Picasso exhibit, I remembered the first time we'd visited the Art Institute, years earlier, and spent a few minutes in front of another of the Spaniard's works, the painting *The Old Guitarist*. Completed perhaps a year before *The Frugal Meal*, the canvas depicts a similarly gaunt man, legs folded, head bowed, his long, thin fingers across his instrument's strings and around its neck. The sorrow it expresses is palpable.

Like a couple other of Picasso's Blue Period works, modern conservation efforts revealed hidden layers beneath *The Old Guitarist*. The earlier paintings found under the visible image include at least two different compositions containing seated women, a child, and an animal. What's not known is whether their obscurity was the result of frugality on Picasso's part, or dissatisfaction with his own work.

Even a modern master's efforts could not completely conceal the presence of those ghost images. Once committed to canvas, they couldn't evade detection indefinitely. Our best efforts at regeneration don't undo what's been done. Subsequent variations and exhibitions build atop the old, but don't oblit-erate it. Whether paintings or wooden grandstands, our old works don't ever disappear completely. Stubborn traces remain, whether physical or psychic, indelible betrayers of those past versions repurposed as the foundations of what's there now, and whatever's to come.

FIELD WORK

On groundskeeping and coaching

The head coach, Dave, arrives first. I'm a couple minutes behind. Dave's already unlocked the shed and rolled out the line chalker. The grass is freshly cut and somebody from the city has dragged the infield with a screen pulled behind a pickup truck. The field looks pretty good, but we'll do a little more gardening before game time.

It's 5:30—ninety minutes before the first pitch of a game under the lights on a warm, soft evening in May. The contesting sides are both comprised of fourteen-year-old boys playing competitive ball in the Eastern Ontario Baseball Association. Our team bears the designation Tier 2, meaning, in the Peterborough Tigers' program, that there's a first team of boys the same age playing at a slightly more competitive level. It's not unusual, when playing teams from the more heavily populated Greater Toronto Area, to encounter Tier 3 or even Tier 4 sides.

Our boys—a baker's dozen of players at varying stages of physical maturity, tall kids and short kids, skinny kids and burly farm kids—will arrive over the course of the next half hour. We'll get them into warm-ups about an hour before the game starts. Before then, though, we are solely dedicated to field prep.

The work is both service and ritual. Preparing our home field requires slowness and patience. We focus on the quality of the dirt on the front of the mound, the groove marks where the infield meets the outfield grass, and the ratio of sand, silt, and clay in the mix of dirt. If there'd been baseball in Japan a thousand years ago, they wouldn't have had to invent the Zen garden; groundskeeping would have sufficed.

The shed, located beyond the first-base dugout, is an unlit concrete rectangle. An incomplete inventory of its contents includes several sets of bases, including clean, firm ones, weather-beaten ones, and soft ones for younger age groups; a couple dragging tools, one an articulated sheet of linked metal squares and the other a wooden frame with nails driven into it; two rakes; about a half-dozen sacks of powdered chalk, a couple of which have inevitably been torn open, some of their contents spilling into snowy drifts; a few bags of red clay for infield repair jobs; an L-screen, disassembled and hanging out of its carrying bag; a couple of baseballs, dirty and ragged. All of it appears to have been tossed haphazardly into the shed. The field's several groups of users—us, the older teams, a house league—don't generally encounter one another, so everybody's content to make a mess and blame it on somebody else if confronted.

In the infield, square metal sleeves are buried in the ground at the location of each base. When nobody's playing baseball, the sleeves are supposed to be plugged with little mushroom-shaped doohickeys that keep the bases' locations visible and prevent dirt from filling the sleeves when it rains or when the infield is dragged. Whoever last used the field didn't bother to replace the plugs, though, so we have to hunt for the sleeves by probing the ground with our cleats. When we find the holes, they are, of course, packed with earth.

Luckily, the spatula's in the shed. It's not actually a spatula, but it looks like one, albeit too thin to flip a pancake. It's exactly the size of one side of the earthbound sleeve. I'm fond of items like this, with extremely specific uses. This one is purpose-built for the highly specialized job of digging dirt out of a dirt-filled square metal tube so you can drop first base into its proper spot.

Though "proper spot" is a misnomer, because the bases at our home diamond, which are supposed to rest ninety feet apart, don't. I've measured them and discovered they're closer to eighty-six feet. The first time we went looking for the post-holes it took an unreasonable amount of time to find them, because we were looking in the right places when we should have been looking in the wrong ones.

Having used the spatula to clean out the sleeves, the bases slot perfectly into position, sitting square to one another, clean white chiclets that'll soon be raced toward by desperate runners and defenders, stomped on by cleated feet, grabbed by gloved hands. Once we're sure they rest snug to the dirt, we pop the bases back out and lay them aside. We have to draw the lines first.

Lying on the floor of the shed, jammed behind a shovel, is an eighteen-inch piece of a hockey stick, affixed with a string and meant to be used as a guide to draw the baselines. Dave digs it out. He drives a six-inch metal pin into the ground at home plate, winds the end of the string around it a few times, and then unspools the string down the length of the infield dirt to where it meets the outfield grass. Using a hammer, he drives a pin into the grass where the painted outfield foul line begins. Then he walks back to the chalker. Making sure the cord is straight and the chalker basin is full, Dave stands at home, pulls the lever to open the device's aperture, and begins to walk slowly from home plate toward first. The chalker drops its soft talc in a four-inch-wide stream onto the smooth reddish-brown dirt. I walk backwards, facing the machine and watching his line, offering correction when necessary.

More of our players have arrived now, hanging their equipment bags from hooks along the back wall of the dugout and jogging out to the field to play a bit of soft toss. The other two coaches, Jake and Keith, have arrived too, and Jake begins to trace the batter's box using a wooden template we rigged up. He places the wood frame down and uses a finger to draw twin three-by-six-foot rectangles in the dirt, four inches off the plate. Meanwhile, with the first-base line drawn, Dave drops the post into the sleeve. The base snugs correctly against the outside edge of the line, a satisfying fit and confirmation that he's laid down a true boundary. I take the string and pin over to shallow left, hammer the spike into the turf, and then walk ahead of Dave once more as he lays down the third-base line. When that's done, he drops third base into place and wheels the chalker homeward to trace Jake's boxes while I head toward shallow right to get warm-ups started.

The boys jog the warning track as I measure off distances—twenty, thirty, fifty, sixty-and-a-half, and ninety feet—dropping orange cones at each. Our players line up along the line at the first cone and begin moving en masse toward the fifty-foot mark, performing an established routine of knee hugs, lunges, arm circles, and other stretches. Then they pick up their gloves and grab balls from a bucket to begin interval throwing. I head back to the infield to rake some dirt.

Good infield dirt is a mixture of sand, clay, and silt. In big-league parks it's about 60 percent sand and 40 percent clay-silt. Nearly all MLB parks source their dirt—a proprietary blend containing Pittsburgh red bed clay, dug from the Glenshaw Formation, where the claystone sits beneath sandstone, gray shale, and limestone—from the same outfit in Pennsylvania. The claystone—favoured by groundskeepers because it will absorb water without swelling—is crushed and mixed in precise proportions with the other constituent material, then shipped to stadiums where it's dumped, pushed, graded, smoothed, and watered until it becomes a perfect surface, one that will neither trip up a runner nor alter the path of a ball.

The pros' mix has a high clay content because in major-league stadiums the infield is watered regularly to keep the clay soft. Your local field isn't likely to get that level of tender loving care, so there's more sand, maybe as much as three quarters of the total fill, though the U14 Tigers have played on fields where the dirt is almost entirely silicate, resulting in a surface that's difficult to run on and that swallows ground balls. Some infields are too silty, which is a problem in a moderate wind or after a player slides, kicking up thick clouds that hang in the air. Too much clay and the sun will bake it into a hardtop surface on which players will be disinclined to slide. These diamonds can make it feel like you're playing baseball on a schoolyard basketball court, giving big bounces and bigger bruises.

Our infield is a bit on the hard side but nowhere near the worst I've seen. It does tend to bake out a bit, especially on the mound, so I use a rake to loosen up the dirt in front of the rubber to make for softer landings. I do the same in the areas around second and third base where players are going to slide, breaking up knots in the tillage. Finally, I rake the borders, the transition point from dirt to grass, and take a quick look for egregious clumps anywhere on the diamond, grooming to make as uniform a surface as I can, given the limits of time and equipment.

After throwing, the boys grab their bats and take turns lobbing each other weighted balls and wiffle balls to get some swings in. There's also a tee and a net that Keith has set up on the other side of the fence, between our dugout and bullpen, and before the first pitch or while waiting to bat during the game, some of our guys will head over there to take cuts.

The lines drawn and the chalker stowed in the shed, Dave's in the dugout writing out the lineup card. Keith's sitting next to him, plugging the lineup into the phone app we use to keep score and tabulate stats. The parents are settling in and our opponents have taken up residence in the third-base dugout. Their warm-ups, all but identical to ours, are underway down the left-field line.

The electronic scoreboard beyond the fence in left-centre blinks to life, and music burbles from a cordless Bluetooth speaker DJed by our backup catcher's parents. Before long a pair of umpires arrive, standing in quiet conference behind our dugout.

Jake and I jog out to gather the orange cones while our players congregate around Keith and Dave near first base. Dave says a few words before he announces the lineup, which we punctuate by double-clapping between each name. The starting catcher dons his gear, and he and the starting pitcher make their way to the fenced-in bullpen for their final pregame warm-up.

Jake takes a bat and a bucket of balls to right and Keith puts on his mitt. The outfielders, both starters and reserves, line up in centre and take turns fielding Jake's fly balls and line drives and then throwing them back to Keith.

The infielders line up in the apron of dirt near our dugout, in foul territory. Dave stands with his bat and I with my mitt. He whacks grounders to boys crouched and ready, who scoop the balls up and whistle throws back to me. These drills are so rhythmic and repetitious that they feel like they'll go on indefinitely, but game time approaches.

At about ten to seven, the umps call the coaches to home plate. Dave jogs over to shake hands with our opponents' head coach and to get a rundown of ground rules and any special instructions the umps might want to share. The governing body's rules require the home team to provide game balls, so Dave brings three fresh pearls from our supply. The rest of us congregate in our dugout, opening bags of dill pickle and sweet chili heat sunflower seeds and filling our pockets. We line up batting helmets in the nine cubbies on the wall and hang bats just below them.

The batting order is written on a small whiteboard that clips onto the dugout fence. The floor crunches with old seed shells. The boys joke, plan their hypothetical home-run celebrations. Us assistant coaches talk about the weather. A couple of kids are applying eye black to their cheeks in ornate lines and shapes more fantastical than functional. Look good, feel good, play good.

When Dave jogs back from the home-plate summit, he says, "Okay, listen up, boys, umpy says he won't give pitchers any warnings on balks, so be careful." Then he delivers some last-minute words of inspiration. The players crowd into a circle and put their hands in the middle. Our starting pitcher leads the cheer, shouting in a voice at once coarse and squeaky, "Tigers on three!" He counts them in and they all cry "Tigers!" before charging out to take the field.

The fielders toss balls around for a few minutes while the pitcher throws his warm-ups. Before long, the umpire tells the catcher, "Two more." The catcher yells out to his fielders, "Balls in!" and all extra balls are tossed toward our dugout where they're collected by one of the kids on the bench. Before the last practice pitch, the catcher shouts, "Coming down!" and once he's caught the toss he pops up, our second baseman cheats toward his bag, and the catcher casts a low arcing throw that hits the two-bagger's glove on the fly. The second baseman slaps down a phantom tag, we all say "Nice toss," or "Good chuck," and the infielders send the ball around the horn before tossing it back to the pitcher.

"Batter," says the umpire, and our opponent's leadoff hitter takes a couple practice swings, strides to the plate, and digs in.

Our starter rears back and delivers the opening salvo, a called strike. The home plate ump addresses the field ump, who's in the grass just beyond first base. "First pitch," says home plate.

The field ump checks his watch. "Seven-oh-one," he shouts back.

"First pitch: seven-oh-one," says home plate, and the official start time is recorded.

The innings fly by in an exuberance of ground balls, sharply hit liners, strikeouts looking. It's suddenly late, and I stand in the third-base coach's box realizing that the sun's golden death throes have given way to a powdery dusk, pink and purple and blue air grown thick with shadflies hatched in the shallows of the nearby Otonabee River, comma-shaped vibrations darting and landing and darting again beneath the lights flaring atop tall metal poles. One fly lands on my shoulder and I leave it there. Another brushes my leg.

Our coach's boxes are not boxes at all, nothing like you see in a major-league game. We never bother to chalk them out; ours are only vague areas of foul territory where the grass is more heavily trampled. We don't invest the care in our spaces that we do the players'. There's something less precious about a coach's box than there is a mound, a batter's box, the place where infield dirt becomes outfield grass.

Most of what we do in our roles as coaches is preparatory in nature, laying the groundwork for things to come. Combing dirt, worrying over the length of grass. The games to be played, the lives to be lived. Tending, planning, guiding. The games don't happen if the field's not ready. The lines need to be painted. Somebody has to write out the lineup. Somebody needs to remind a kid standing on third to tag up on a ball hit in the air. It might as well be us.

VEECK AS IN VEECK

On Bill Veeck and work-life balance

In May 1952, Bill Veeck and his family moved into Sportsman's Park. It made perfect sense, as he had grown up in a ballpark himself.

His father, William Louis Veeck, Sr., was a sportswriter in Chicago who wrote under the pseudonym Bill Bailey, and who was so critical of Cubs owner William Wrigley that Wrigley offered him a shot to do better by the club. Eventually Veeck Sr. did, securing two pennants (though no titles). By the time he was about ten, Veeck the younger was helping out around the stadium that would eventually bear Wrigley's name. Young Bill tore tickets and sold concessions. He went away to school but returned when his father fell ill. Once home, Bill took a job with the Cubs under Philip K. Wrigley, who'd succeeded his own father.

Bill and P. K. mixed like chalk and cheese. Bill made suggestions and Wrigley rejected them, though among the lasting marks of Veeck's time with the Cubs was the ivy he helped to plant at the base of the park's brick outfield wall. He also, alongside long-time associate Harry Grabiner, organized the city's ballpark vendors into a union. In his autobiography, *Veeck as in Wreck*, he wrote that he and Grabiner organized the vendors so that folks hawking peanuts and beer would "be guaranteed a living wage and the clubs would be guaranteed a professional working force."

The situation with the Cubs became untenable. Veeck left the team, determined to make his own way in the game. He was young, recently married to circus performer Eleanor Raymond, and full of ideas. Using charm, hustle, and other people's money—which would become his MO going forward—he purchased the Milwaukee Brewers of the American Association, then a Double A league, in 1941.

"I was twenty-eight years old," Veeck wrote. "I had a wife and two children. I was dead broke. But I had my ball club and a bountiful belief that I was going to make the baseball world sit up and take notice."

He got to work right away. He installed Charlie Grimm, a co-investor, as manager, then cleaned and repainted Borchert Field ("an architectural monstrosity," according to Veeck), and stood at the gate to welcome fans as they arrived. Once the turnstiles stopped spinning, the Brewers had drawn their largest crowd in years.

People continued to come, but money remained tight. Turns out it's expensive to run a baseball team. Veeck concocted an elaborate patchwork of improvised solutions, mainly involving short-term loans and the sale of players. Meanwhile, Borchert Field was becoming his sandbox—if he could dream it, he'd do it. He scheduled morning games to cater to shift workers. He gave away farm animals. For Grimm's birthday, Veeck loaded a left-handed pitcher into a cardboard cake.

He sat in the stands and frequented the bars the fans drank in so he could listen to his customers. He talked to cabbies and waiters. He shook hands, gave away tickets, contributed to charitable causes. He spoke to any organization, club, or gathering willing to have him. Veeck also invited the ire of his fellow American Association team owners for innovations such as a screen atop the right-field fence that moved into and out of position via hydraulic motor.

Veeck's wheeling and dealing wasn't simply aimed at filling seats and grabbing headlines—he improved the product on the field too. He worked the phones and turned over every rock to find the players Grimm needed. The Brewers couldn't salvage the 1941 season, with the club finishing last in the eight-team circuit, but they vaulted to second in 1942 and then went on a run, claiming the next three American Association pennants.

Veeck missed most of it. After the 1943 season, he enlisted in the Marines and was sent to the Pacific, where an accident shattered his right leg. He remained in a hospital bed for the remainder of the war.

When at last he returned stateside, he had to heal both his body and his relationship. Things with Eleanor had been on the rocks since he signed up for active duty, and upon his return home he had a choice to make. He chose his marriage, sold the Brewers, and the family entrenched at a ranch in Arizona.

But the marriage couldn't be saved, and in time Bill made his way back to baseball. In 1946, he assembled a group and engaged in some creative financing to buy the hard-luck American League club in Cleveland. Bill assumed the reins and began putting the stunts, shenanigans, promotions, campaigns, and schemes he'd developed with the Brewers—including a modifiable outfield fence—to work in the majors. Attendance rose substantially and the ballclub's place in the standings rose slightly. Then things started to happen.

Veeck signed Larry Doby in 1947, and the young outfielder integrated the AL only a few months after Jackie Robinson crossed the colour line in the NL. In 1948, Veeck signed forty-something Satchel Paige, a Negro Leagues legend who, though he'd played thousands of pro and amateur games across several hemispheres, was new to white major-league ball, and so qualified as the oldest rookie ever to take a major-league field.

Paige's presence was no mere stunt—the ageless hurler was instrumental to the 1948 team's success, an entertaining and dependable bullpen fixture, and a showman who still threw strikes. Shortstop-manager Lou Boudreau turned in a career year, and starters Bob Lemon and Bob Feller combined for 39 wins. The team claimed its first pennant since 1920, followed by something the Forest City has not, as of this writing, had since: a World Series championship. The team spent fifteen years splitting its home dates between old, intimate League Park and the cavernous new Municipal Stadium until Veeck moved the team permanently to the larger venue and proceeded to pack it. During the 1948 World Series, games four and five each drew in excess of eighty thousand fans.

For Veeck, however, life intervened to force him out of baseball once more. Eleanor filed for divorce in 1949 and, so he could pay her what she was fairly owed, Bill had to sell his stake in the club. But Veeck had tasted success in the big leagues, and Cleveland wouldn't be his last stop on the circuit.

★★★

Bill Veeck was easy to identify in a crowd. A casual dresser—*The Sporting News* frequently referred to him simply as "Sport Shirt"—he moved about with the aid of crutches and, after his injured leg was amputated above the knee, a wooden leg. He was dynamic, outgoing, and unable to keep still.

Veeck envisioned the game as the entertainment and rooting passion of working-class people, offering affordable tickets. When Cleveland earned a spot in the World Series, Veeck made it possible to buy a ticket to a single game, where previously fans shelled out for passes to all games played in a team's park. He also ensured there was plenty of beer, music, fireworks, and goofy spectacle alongside the action between the foul lines.

It's remarkable that a person could own and run a Major League Baseball team, and yet somehow give off the signals of middle-class normalcy. Veeck did a thing he loved, and it was hard, and tiring, and financially precarious, but he kept doing it for others like him who also loved baseball. In the circles he ran in, and the world that's come since, that everyman-ness was, and remains, utterly singular.

It was fitting in a way that twists of fortune would next bring Veeck to St. Louis—home of old von der Ahe, he of the beer garden and cheap tickets. Once again the face of a sizeable investors' group, Veeck would buy the Browns.

Fellow AL owners were concerned that Veeck planned to acquire the Browns only to move them to another market, but he denied it and said his intention was to force the Cardinals out of town. In those pre-expansion days, five cities hosted multiple big-league teams. Of those five, only Boston was smaller than St. Louis. On top of that, the Browns and Cardinals continued to share Sportsman's Park. With television threatening to eat into crowds and families fleeing downtown for the suburbs, Veeck knew the city wouldn't comfortably accommodate both teams for long. His one shot, he figured, was to out-dazzle the Cardinals as a means of winning the hearts of the fans. He was busy executing the plan—cleaning and repainting the ballpark, signing Paige again, and, in one memorable promotion, letting the crowd make managerial decisions—when Cards owner Fred Saigh was thrown in jail and forced to sell his team.

Enter Gussie Busch and his ample, sudsy resources. Understanding the odds had shifted against him, Veeck petitioned to move the Browns to Baltimore. The other AL owners were not Veeck fans—his latest and arguably most heinous crime had been to suggest that all teams should receive an equal portion of national TV rights money—and they voted him down. In the end, he sold to a Baltimore-based group who did just what he'd proposed. The Browns were no more and Bill Veeck was out of baseball once again.

★★★

In 1950, Bill married Mary Frances Ackerman, a one-time PR specialist for the Ice Capades who was able to match Bill's freak. She remained patient and flexible in the wake of the Browns' sale while he cast about looking for his next opportunity. He made a run at getting a team in California before the Giants and Dodgers relocated, tried to buy a circus, did some scouting, some TV work, dabbled in the minors again. Then a death in the Comiskey dynasty created an opening, and he assembled a group to buy a majority stake in the White Sox. Under his watch, Comiskey Park crowds swelled, and in 1959, the Sox took their first pennant in forty years. They lost the Series to the freshly transplanted Dodgers, but things still looked good on the South Side.

And then the Sox slid back to the middle of the American League pack in the following seasons and Veeck's health declined, forcing him to sell once again—though not before giving the world another innovation: the famous exploding scoreboard, which featured flashing lights, pinwheels, and fireworks.

Once his health allowed, Veeck ventured out into the world, a hustler looking for a hustle. He ran a pony track, did some more TV, tried without luck to buy other teams. He also published his autobiography, making more enemies in the process, and kept talking on TV and in the papers about the fools and misers who still owned baseball teams. Which made it a small miracle when, in 1975, the aforementioned owners approved his bid to buy back the White Sox.

It was his last hurrah. The world was changing and the days of men like Veeck operating major-league teams were all but over. Free agency was rewriting the rules; it was going to cost more and more to run a baseball team, far more than an ordinary businessperson could manage. But Sport Shirt wouldn't leave baseball without making his mark one last time. He put his team in short pants and butterfly collars, and donned a peg leg to recreate Archibald Willard's painting *The Spirit of '76*. He hired his son, Mike, and eventually gave him the title of director of promotions. And on July 12, 1979, with Mike's help, Bill staged Disco Demolition Night, perhaps the most infamous promotion in the history of baseball.

The goal was to score relevance with young people, grab headlines for the team, and sell a bunch of tickets. During a doubleheader with the Tigers, fans who brought disco records with them would pay reduced admission. The records would be collected and, between games, a huge pile of them would be blown to high heaven. It was perhaps cynical, given the racial dynamics of a bunch of young, largely white kids, many of whom had little interest in baseball, figuratively and literally destroying racialized music. But in the cold terms of an attention economy, it worked. The place was full—nearly 48,000 paid customers, with more turned away, for a Thursday night home game for the eleventh-best team in the American League.

When it came time for the pyrotechnics, chaos erupted. The explosion tore a crater in the playing surface. Thousands of fans overran the field, climbed the foul poles, pulled up chunks of turf, hurled records like frisbees into the densely packed stands, and made off with bats and bases. The Chicago PD arrived in riot gear and made thirty-nine arrests. Due to damage to the field, the second scheduled game was forfeited to the Tigers.

Mike Veeck, who was twenty-eight years old at the time, stood rooted to a spot near second base as the madness unfolded. "I was just standing there thinking about what my next job would be," he later said.

Already a pariah among fellow owners, Bill Veeck became persona non grata in the wake of the disaster. This, along with the new financial reality of post-reserve clause baseball and his further declining health, forced him out of baseball for good. He held out for a couple of years, but in 1981 he sold the White Sox to a group led by Jerry Reinsdorf, a lawyer turned real estate tycoon, and a kind of anti-Veeck who entered sports ownership after making over $100 million by selling his property investment firm. Reinsdorf is exemplary of the new breed of team owner, the kind that would render Veeck's model completely unworkable. As of this writing, Reinsdorf still owns the team, as well as the National Basketball Association's Chicago Bulls.

★★★

When Bill Veeck followed his father into baseball, the game was a cottage industry—popular, I grant, but not at all resembling the multibillion-dollar sports-entertainment sector the game is today. When Bill was shown the exit, the possibility of anyone of modest means sitting at the big table at MLB owners' meetings departed along with him.

Bill Veeck came at things differently. Before asking if a stunt would turn a profit, he always asked if it would be fun. He gave away animals, trips, cars. He gave away a thousand cupcakes—to one person. He did likewise with a thousand cans of beer, explaining, "To give one can of beer to a thousand people is not nearly as much fun as to give 1,000 cans of beer to one guy… You give a thousand cans to one guy, and there is always an outside possibility that 50,000 people will talk about it." He didn't seek to align with or curry the favour of fellow owners, but instead sought communion with fans and players—the relationships that mattered. He cared about what fans wanted because he remained a fan. His teams weren't assets in a wider portfolio. They were his consuming passion.

Veeck's appeal lies in his being the last regular person to own a team, a feat he accomplished with other people's money and his own spit, elbow grease, and hustle. He brought a championship to Cleveland, integrated the American League, brought Satchel Paige to the white major leagues and then kept employing him. Those three acts would be legacy enough, but Veeck was disliked by the sorts of people who owned baseball teams, and that strikes me as a pretty good test of character in its own right. When Veeck left baseball for the last time, the door slammed shut behind him, and the fact that no one could ever again do what he did is proof that the billionaires have stolen the game from us for good.

There is legal ownership and there is moral ownership. In the modern baseball era, legally, the deed to your favourite team belongs to oligarchs and pharma billionaires and oil brats. You can look it up; the information is a matter of public record. Morally, it's you and me who put up the real stakes, placing our very hearts on the line 162 times a year. Maybe we're fools for cheering for someone else's hybrid legal entity that extracts profit from the men getting their uniforms dirty. We probably are. But of all the dummies and privileged inheritors to have possessed a professional baseball team, Veeck alone might be mistaken for one of us. He sat in the stands and drank beer. He blistered beneath a too-hot sun, he grew hoarse from screaming, he bore grudges, and he used the power he'd accumulated to help players who were easy to cheer for—guys who'd made mistakes, guys who were over the hill, guys who needed one last shot.

Bill Veeck died of lung cancer in 1986, but I feel a high degree of confidence in saying that he would have hated regional sports networks. He would have despised AI-powered statistical collection and analysis, instant replay, and umps checking pitchers for sticky stuff after every inning. He'd have decried the coming dawn of robot umps, because Bill Veeck lived in the creases of ambiguity, in the places where facts bow to feelings. His domain was the specious and the questionable. The gloriously, demonstrably false. The poor taste and the popular choice.

We're all in the teeth of this thing; the marks press deep into our skin. We love what we love while hating those who control it. But Bill Veeck was the last to sneak inside the machine and steer it. He'd hang on until he was spit out, and then he'd find his way back in again. Veeck saw beauty and knew he wanted to share it. He knew a baseball team was yours as much as it was his.

Bill Veeck may have been broken and incomplete, but he was all effort. And he made baseball fun. All the weird, silly, stupid things that make you smile at a ballgame—the hot dogs dropped in parachutes, the eyeball races, the dizzy bat races, the giveaways, the contests, the pranks and prizes—were touched by him. Thanks to Veeck, a night at the ballpark today is equal parts contest and carnival, because his stamp is all over the contemporary experience of taking in a game. Making all nine innings feel like a departure from our real lives with cash drops, giveaways, theme nights—that's all him.

Veeck moved his family into Sportsman's Park. His kids' backyard was the outfield, and he slept where he toiled, seventy years before work from home was a thing. There was no work-life balance. His work *was* life. The game was work and work a game. There was no other world, no separate place. The lines weren't blurred—they didn't exist at all.

IT WOULD BE A SHAMBLES

On Curt Flood, the reserve clause, free agency, and the private jet that Shohei Ohtani was not actually on

I first used a flight tracking website on a Friday afternoon in December 2023. I wasn't alone; speculation concerning the purpose of the voyage and identity of the passengers aboard was pinging all over the internet. People whose interest ranged from boredom-induced curiosity to outright mania followed along, for anywhere from a few minutes to a few hours, to verify that this plane did exist and would, at roughly 4:30 p.m. EST, touch down in the early winter gloaming of Toronto Pearson International Airport, about twenty kilometres west of the Rogers Centre.

The flight was purported to be carrying Shohei Ohtani, the most sought-after free agent in baseball, certainly of that offseason and maybe of all time. According to "insiders" and "well-placed industry sources," the dots could possibly, conceivably be connected in such a way to suggest that the purpose of this trip was to sign a very large contract with the Blue Jays.

Ohtani was used to being pursued. When the Hokkaido Nippon-Ham Fighters posted him following the 2017 Nippon Professional Baseball season, he was twenty-three years old and had already won the Japan Series, been a five-time NPB

All-Star, won MVP of the Pacific League and an ERA title, and been named both the best hitter and the best pitcher in Japan. He was a unicorn, a mythical being whose existence seemed both impossible and too tantalizing to dismiss. The Yankees, Rangers, Dodgers, Cubs, Mariners, Padres, Giants, and Twins were believed to be in dogged pursuit. It was something of a surprise when Ohtani chose the Los Angeles Angels from among all these suitors—"he felt a true bond" with the team, according to his agent.

Six seasons, one Rookie of the Year award, two MVPs, three All-Star selections, one home-run title, two Silver Sluggers, and a Commissioner's Historic Achievement Award later, that bond, and his contract with the Angels, expired (owing, perhaps, to one more striking number: zero playoff games played). Ohtani was a free agent, and it was widely assumed he would sign the largest contract in baseball history. There were other free agents that winter—Cody Bellinger, Blake Snell, Matt Chapman—but the only player whose employment status registered outside of the baseball world was Ohtani. He would certainly draw the first half-billion dollar contract in the history of the game—but how much more than that, and where he'd sign, drew interest from the mainstream press. That Toronto, traditionally viewed as a hard sell to big free agents by virtue of its location, was even in the conversation was remarkable. And for Blue Jays fans, it was electrifying.

Ohtani, some frenzied and partial observers felt, would slide into the DH position on a team that already featured young stars Vladimir Guerrero Jr. and Bo Bichette, along with a strong pitching rotation anchored by Kevin Gausman and Chris Bassitt. Ohtani would provide offence in 2024 and beyond. By 2025, he'd have recovered from his second Tommy John surgery to return to the mound, where he'd essentially double his value. Atop that, his enormous profile in Japan would help the Blue Jays become more attractive to Asian fans. Whatever the outlay—and talk had the necessary terms rising to ten years and $600 million or more—it would prove a money-making move for Rogers Communications Inc., the telecom company that owns the team.

Internet sleuths quickly spread rumours that the Jays' extant Japanese-born player, lefty Yusei Kikuchi—a high school teammate of Ohtani's—had made a reservation for a large party at a downtown Toronto sushi restaurant on the same day we were tracking the plane. Clearly, a celebration was planned.

Amid all this breathless anticipation, it became easy to believe that shortly after that plane landed, the world's best baseball player would be standing behind a podium, pulling on a Blue Jays jersey, and posing for photos. So, like countless other Jays fans, I watched and waited for him to emerge onto the tarmac.

★★★

Things were very different for ballplayers in 1969. Just ask Curt Flood.

Flood was a Gold Glove centre fielder for the Cardinals with some pop in his bat and few holes in his swing. Flood hit .300 or better six times and helped the Cardinals win the World Series in 1964 and 1967, and the National League pennant in 1968. He was a three-time All-Star, the Cardinals' co-captain, and in 1968 *Sports Illustrated* called him "Baseball's Best Center Fielder"—high praise in the era of Willie Mays.

Flood's *Sporting News* card notes his race in neat type at the top of the card, marking him as among the first wave of

Black stars to have begun their professional careers in Major League Baseball. By contrast, Satchel Paige's card does not mention race, nor does Don Newcombe's, though the latter does mention Newk's time with the Newark Eagles of the Negro National League, while Paige's entry says nothing of his long and winding road through every form of professional, semi-professional, international, and unofficial baseball prior to his arrival in Cleveland in the summer of 1948. Tantalizingly, Paige's card does feature a telephone number.

Flood and the Cardinals finished nine games clear of the Giants in 1968, setting up a World Series clash with Detroit, the cream of the American League. The teams split the first six games, requiring a deciding match in St. Louis.

Game Seven was a pitchers duel, with the Tigers' Mickey Lolich and the Cards' Bob Gibson trading a string of scoreless innings. With two outs in the seventh, the score knotted at zero and two Tigers on base, Detroit outfielder Jim Northrup hit a sharp liner to centre. Flood broke quickly in, but realized it was heading over his head, reversed course, and temporarily lost his footing, which cost him a step. The ball sailed over him and rolled to the wall, where it came to rest. Flood picked it up and fired it in, but by the time the ball reached the infield Northrup was already standing at third and two runs had scored. The scorer ruled it a clean triple, which looks about right; the only reason Flood made it as close a play as he did was because he was Curt Flood. Most fielders never would have had a chance on that hit.

The Cardinals couldn't mount a concerted attack on Lolich—just a solo shot by Mike Shannon in the bottom of the ninth. Lolich hung in long enough to get Tim McCarver to pop out to the catcher for the final out, giving the Tigers' durable lefty his third win of the Series and earning him the title of the Classic's MVP.

Flood had gone 2-for-4 with a stolen base in Game Seven, in addition to being picked off first and getting a bad jump on Northrup's liner. In the Series he hit .286 (8-for-28), drove in two, scored four, and was 3-for-3 stealing bases, while playing errorless defence.

Nevertheless, the public, and perhaps to a greater extent Cardinals owner Gussie Busch, blamed Flood for the loss, and though Flood had turned in a stellar season—he was named an All-Star, won a Gold Glove, and finished fourth in MVP voting—Busch offered his fleet fielder only a modest raise that offseason. The strict letter of the contract's reserve clause decreed that the team could exercise broad discretion on whether to keep the ballplayer or cut him loose, and how much they were willing to pay him. The player had considerably less choice: sign or quit baseball. In Flood's case, the team, in the person of Busch, wished to retain his services, and to do so had only to offer a contract. Flood had in mind a figure of $90,000 for 1969, while Busch's offer was $77,500. The two sides eventually settled at Flood's figure before he reported to spring training, but the previously cordial relationship between player and owner was unquestionably damaged.

In spring training, Busch gathered Cardinals' staff, his brewery higher-ups, and the St. Louis beat writers to sit in on a meeting with the players, then proceeded to lay into his club, suggesting they were greedy, unfocused, and lacked dedication. In *The Way It Is*, the autobiography Flood co-wrote with Richard Carter, Flood indicated that the owner's lecture "demoralized the 1969 Cardinals."

The negative feeling lingered; the Cardinals won only eighty-seven games, the Mets won one hundred, and St. Louis fell to fourth in the new National League East division. Flood continued to provide sparkling defence in centre field, winning another Gold Glove, but his offensive production slipped a notch.

Not a week after the regular season ended, Flood got a phone call from Jim Toomey, general manager Bing Devine's assistant, with the news that he'd been traded to the Phillies.

Not only was Flood disinclined to go to Philadelphia—he felt the city was essentially racist, and that the organization was cheap and poorly run—but he believed his fourteen years of major-league experience should allow him some say in his fate. As things stood, his options were to accept the trade (Phils GM Bob Quinn, no relation to the Browns executive of the same name, indicated the club would offer Flood $100,000 for the 1970 season) or retire. Both were out of the question in Flood's mind. He needed a third option.

He called Marvin Miller.

Miller was a labour negotiator with a degree in economics, the Bronx-born son of a Russian émigré. He'd worked for the US Treasury Department, the New York City welfare department, the International Association of Machinists, the United Auto Workers, and the United Steelworkers. Miller was a working man's man. Dapper and cool tempered, he wore a thin moustache that frequently framed a wry, knowing smile.

Miller came to the head of the Major League Baseball Players Association in 1966 after a fractious vote. During the process, a smear campaign by team owners and execs suggested the first thing Miller would do was orchestrate a strike, an ordeal most rank-and-file ballplayers couldn't weather financially.

Miller had no such plan in mind. He'd assumed the reins of a toothless union—the latest of several attempts to organize ballplayers in order to maximize their leverage and make the experience of playing big-league baseball easier, better, and more equitable for superstars and bench jockeys alike. John Montgomery Ward's Brotherhood of Professional Base Ball Players had succeeded briefly in 1889, but when the Players' League fell apart after its lone season in 1890, the Brotherhood died with it. Several other associations enjoyed brief existences, winning small concessions from owners such as a spring training per diem, a league-wide minimum salary, limits on the size of pay cuts year over year, and the establishment of a pension fund. Owners continued to hold all the cards but would occasionally deign to selectively placate players' demands.

Pensions were the players' source of greatest concern when Miller took office. The existing program was underfunded and poorly managed, and Miller resolved to shore up the fund. But he also recognized that each one of the players' justifiable grievances paled in importance next to the need to defeat the reserve clause once and for all.

In Flood, Miller saw the perfect person to challenge the hated rule, and he offered Flood the financial backing of the MLBPA if he chose to pursue the case. Flood accepted the offer, and he and Miller got to work. Their opening salvo was a letter to Commissioner Bowie Kuhn. "After twelve years in the major leagues," it opened, "I do not feel that I am a piece of property to be bought and sold." Flood requested that the commissioner inform all teams that he was available to sign a contract to play the following season.

Kuhn replied that such a thing was impossible. Flood sued Kuhn, the AL and NL presidents, and the presidents of all twenty-four MLB teams.

The reserve clause had been challenged before. In 1946, Danny Gardella—a good-hitting (at least by the standards of wartime baseball) yet error-prone utility guy—refused what he felt was an insulting contract offer from the Giants, who owned his rights in perpetuity under the rule. Instead, he jumped to the Mexican League. The move earned him a spot on then Commissioner Happy Chandler's blacklist. Gardella filed a lawsuit charging that the clause denied a ballplayer his right to make a living. The suit was rejected by a federal judge who cited the precedent of *Federal Baseball Club v. National League*, but Gardella appealed and was awarded a trial by jury.

The baseball establishment objected. "Without the reserve clause," Branch Rickey told reporters in reference to Gardella's case, "baseball cannot endure." He also suggested that Gardella, and those who supported him, possessed "Communist tendencies."

The economic strain of sustained legal activity eventually got the better of Gardella, who let his lawyer talk him into accepting a settlement offer from the owners.

Flood was determined not to follow Gardella's path. With the backing of the MLBPA, he was prepared for a lengthy process and would accept no settlement short of the end of the reserve clause. It was a steep challenge, and the public was not necessarily on his side. After all, what did a man earning $90,000 a year playing a child's game have to complain about, asked Howard Cosell on ABC's *Wide World of Sports*. Flood responded, "A well-paid slave is nonetheless a slave."

The bench trial, held in Manhattan, lasted three weeks. As in the Gardella case, the game's ruling class circled the wagons. They inferred that the driving force behind the lawsuit was Marvin Miller, not Curt Flood, and that it amounted to a heavy-handed negotiation tactic. Kuhn said that without the reserve clause, "baseball as we know it simply could not survive." NL president Chub Feeney suggested that the only factor preserving the integrity of the game was the reserve clause. AL president Joe Cronin—who, as a player, had been traded away by his own father-in-law, Clark Griffith—testified for the defence, as did a steady suited parade of baseball executives and insiders. Louis L. Hoynes Jr., doomsayer and attorney for the defence, claimed that if Flood won the case, "it would be a shambles and make impossible and illegal almost any effort to negotiate."

No current players dared to testify on Flood's behalf. Worse, no current player—not even his Cardinals teammates—showed up to watch the trial or offer public support for Flood, even though his was a trial their union dues were paying for.

Flood's willing defenders, however, were an impressive bunch. Jackie Robinson, white haired and diabetic, railed against the clause, and called Flood courageous. Hank Greenberg, who had the unique experience of being both a superstar player and an owner (he'd taken a minority stake in the White Sox with Bill Veeck), said, "I would be perfectly willing to invest in baseball tomorrow if we had no reserve clause." Ex-pitcher Jim Brosnan, who'd effectively been kicked out of baseball for writing a pair of tell-all books about the game, took the stand for the plaintiff. And Veeck himself, after having sold the Sox the first time due to health concerns, spoke enthusiastically against the reserve clause, which he'd once called "legally and morally indefensible" in a letter to Judge Landis. Veeck told the court that players should "have the right to determine their future for themselves." He added, "I think that it would certainly help the players and the game itself to no longer be one of the few places in which there is human bondage."

It wasn't enough. Judge Irving Ben Cooper was not persuaded that the whole system should be dismantled and felt that his hands were tied by earlier rulings. "Clearly," he wrote in his decision, "the preponderance of the credible proof does not favor elimination of the reserve clause." Flood appealed but was denied, and so petitioned the Supreme Court to hear the case. On June 19, 1970, their decision came down: 5–3 against Flood. The court's decision cited the earlier precedent of *Federal Baseball* as binding, barring an act of Congress.

But public perception was shifting. What had been viewed as a natural state of affairs now seemed outdated and unfair to the majority of baseball fans. When the Basic Agreement expired after the 1969 season, the players entered contract negotiations with new bargaining power. Instead of wholly dismantling the existing system, the MLBPA recognized the value of a piecemeal approach. The 1970 deal included an arbitration program for the first time—the system that a few years later allowed Catfish Hunter to be declared a free agent by an arbitrator, the first player with major-league experience to be so named, giving him the opportunity to entertain bids and eventually sign with the Yankees. The ensuing collective agreement, signed after a lockout during spring training in 1973, introduced the Curt Flood rule, the stipulation that after ten years of playing time, and five with their current club, a player would earn the right to veto any potential trade.

The fatal blow to the reserve clause came in 1975. Pitchers Andy Messersmith of the Dodgers and Dave McNally of the Expos both refused to sign their renewed contracts and played that season under the terms of their previous deals. The pitchers argued that the effect would be to render them free agents ahead of the 1976 season. The owners disagreed, but arbitrator Peter Seitz did not, finding that the standard contract bound a player to his club for one year, not forever. The decision was upheld by the courts, and the new collective agreement, signed shortly thereafter, granted players the right of free agency.

There's a short, straight line between Flood's decision to sue baseball's power structure and the modern model in which a player that has accrued six years of playing time at the major-league level may enter into free agency in order to determine his own path.

These changes arrived too late for Flood, though. He never played a game for the Phillies, sitting out all of the 1970 season before the lowly Washington Senators acquired Flood's rights from Philadelphia in another trade. He came to an agreement to play for the Senators in 1971—for $110,000 and a promise that he'd be released at the end of the season if he so chose.

But Flood's time had passed. The rigours of the legal process and time away from the diamond had aged him—he was simply no longer the player he'd been. He played thirteen more games before hanging it up for good, at which point he decamped to Majorca and opened a bar.

★★★

Back to the rumoured plane: it touched down in Toronto, taxied to a hangar, and when the door opened, the figure that emerged was not Ohtani, but rather the businessman who owned the jet.

Internet buzz pivoted to the theory that the flight was a ruse and the Blue Jays were being used by Ohtani's representatives to leverage a bigger contract. In the end, it turned out people were attempting to connect dots that weren't connected and then crowing about it online.

Ohtani was instead at home in Southern California, where he announced the next morning, via an Instagram post, that he was signing with the Dodgers. The ten-year, $700 million deal was the richest in baseball history by a long shot. The contract was creatively structured—most of the money was deferred, leaving plenty of room for the Dodgers to build winning teams around Ohtani, which granted him some measure of control over not only where he played but also the quality of the players he'd toil alongside. "I was just following the news," Ohtani later said in an interview. "I knew I wasn't on that flight, so I was curious too."

The precise contours of what Curt Flood or Marvin Miller envisioned probably hadn't included a Japanese two-way player choosing between multiple contracts in excess of a half-billion dollars and opting to earn most of that money after he retired. But in spirit—a generational talent entertaining offers from multiple willing clubs and then choosing his preferred destination and terms—it was exactly what they'd hoped for. That freedom is what Miller worked for and what Flood ultimately sacrificed his career for others to attain.

Shohei Ohtani was never bodily aboard that airplane. Metaphorically, though, I'd suggest he was there: lofted high, jetting toward just compensation for his value, ascending from the liftoff point of Flood's principled stand, nearing the point where gravity's influence wanes and an object will continue to fly forever.

THE NINTH INNING OF THE SEVENTH GAME

On daytime baseball, the workday, everydayness, and the businessperson's special

Bill Mazeroski's big swing came on a Thursday afternoon. You've likely seen footage: the Pirates' slight second baseman sprinting around first as the ball clears Yogi Berra's head and then the wall in left. Maz, rounding second, his cap in his right hand, begins windmilling his arms. He runs into a mob of well-wishers at third, civilians in street dress who accompany him down the home stretch. At the plate he disappears in a dense assemblage of humanity, some in uniform, some not.

Forbes Field, the Pirates' home from 1909 to 1970 and the site of the aforementioned drama, is gone, but bits of it remain on the verdant campus of the University of Pittsburgh. Home plate is kept under glass, parts of the brick outfield wall still stand, and there's a metal marker set in concrete signifying the spot where Mazeroski's bullet felled the mighty Yankees.

Its patinaed inscription reads:

> THIS MARKS THE SPOT WHERE
> BILL MAZEROSKI'S HOME RUN
> BALL CLEARED THE LEFT CENTER
> FIELD WALL OF FORBES FIELD

ON OCTOBER 13, 1960, THEREBY WINNING THE WORLD SERIES CHAMPIONSHIP FOR THE PITTSBURGH PIRATES
THE HISTORIC HIT CAME IN THE NINTH INNING OF THE SEVENTH GAME TO BEAT THE NEW YORK YANKEES BY A SCORE OF 10–9.

Almost all of the greatest World Series plays that have occurred in my lifetime—Jackson, Puckett, Ortiz, Bumgarner, or Betts—unfolded under artificial light. But wind the 1960 film back and let it play, and you'll see Mazeroski run into shadow as he darts up the first-base line. Watch it now and it hits you like an ice cream headache, all at once: that's *sunshine*. October sunshine, dry and golden as straw, somehow detectable though the black and white of the original broadcast.

The ninth inning of the seventh game of the 1960 World Series was played in the afternoon, as were all World Series games until the fourth game of the 1971 Fall Classic, in which these same Pirates beat the visiting Orioles 4–3 and went on to take the Series in seven.

These days, championships are decided on late October and early November nights under the flattened brilliance of LED lighting systems, live on FOX, with a fast-food chain promotion promising a free taco for every living American if a player steals a base. We've grown so accustomed to the World Series' greatest dramas occurring after midnight Eastern. It's a tall order to imagine a world in which people kicked off work early so they could stand before department store TV displays to watch a few innings before hopping a train home to maybe catch the thrilling end on the living room tube, or on the radio in the kitchen.

It wasn't that Forbes Field couldn't be lit, mind you. Indeed, Maz passes beneath the silhouette of a light tower on his way down the line. That very season, the Pirates played about half their home games at night. Nocturnal baseball was well established in the Steel City. The eight light towers ringing the park were installed in 1940. Three of them were placed in the outfield, their footings squarely within the field of play, standing ready to create havoc should a ball reach them and rattle around within their Erector Set–like bases.

The first night game played at Forbes was ten years before the towers' installation, when the Homestead Grays were tenants at the Bucs' ballyard. On July 18, 1930, the Grays, then operating as an independent team, met the Negro National League's Kansas City Monarchs in a game set to begin at 8:30 p.m. Monarchs owner J. L. Wilkinson had invested in a portable truck-mounted lighting system. The Monarchs were the runaway champs of the NNL the year before but were still struggling at the gate, and the entrepreneurial Wilkinson figured that playing games at night would bring in crowds for whom daylit baseball was inconvenient or impossible, including racialized labourers for whom there was no possibility of attending what was then known as a businessman's special. The four light trucks—each sporting six floodlights atop telescoping fifty-foot poles—and their gasoline-powered generator allowed the Monarchs to entertain opponents on the road or at home at KC's Muehlebach Field. The era of night baseball had begun, and with it an age of barnstorming, both of which would help many teams survive the Depression and countless players maintain a livelihood.

Illumination didn't reach the white majors until 1935, when the Reds first lit up Cincinnati's Crosley Field with a theatrical assist from FDR. In Washington, the president pressed a Western Union telegraph key, sending a signal to Reds president Larry MacPhail in Cincinnati, who then flipped a switch to fire up 632 floodlights arrayed atop Crosley's grandstand. Most other teams followed in fairly short order, with only the Cubs' Wrigley Field holding out until 1988.

But day baseball remained the postseason norm three and a half decades after that night in Cincinnati. Experimentally, the 1967 All-Star Game went prime-time. It drew a decent audience, so the '68 Midsummer Classic happened after the Eastern time zone's dinnertime too. In 1969, the scheduled date for the All-Star Game was rained out, forcing a makeup the next afternoon. The TV ratings crashed.

For Commissioner Bowie Kuhn, the case was made: night ball was the future. He pushed for more events to be held when folks were by and large home from work and school. Game Four of the 1971 Series commenced in the evening, and Kuhn was pleased. "We beat out *All in the Family*," he said, reflecting baseball's dawning awareness that in the postwar world it was the viewers at home, not the fans in the stands, that must be courted, and that the real competition was *Gunsmoke*, not day jobs. The national pastime had become prime-time programming.

Mixing day games and night games remained the practice until 1985, when it was announced that the pennant winners would contest that year's championship entirely by lamplight. The six-year, $1.1 billion national TV deal that Kuhn had signed in 1983 allowed MLB to opt for night games in the league championships and World Series, and Kuhn exercised that right.

That's the world you and I know, of night games, and of sprawling playoff game lengths, combining to push the last out later and later into the night. The last World Series day game occurred on Saturday, October 24, 1987, with Game Six between the Twins and the Cardinals. First pitch was just after 3:00 p.m. local time—indoors, at the Metrodome in Minneapolis. For the record, it was forty degrees Fahrenheit and cloudy outside. The last time the Fall Classic was played outdoors before nightfall was in 1984, when the first pitch of Game Four at Tiger Stadium was thrown at 1:30 p.m. Eastern.

While it lasted, the daytime World Series suggested that baseball is so important that its crowning event merits exceptional treatment, and we'll let it divert our collective attention during work hours.

By 1987, it was clear that the nine-to-five world was being replaced by disparate twenty-four-hour cycles. Stores were open later, and shift work chopped the day into new shapes. Cable news, sports, weather, shopping on Sundays: We didn't know it then, but we were only a few innovations away from a computer that would fit in a pocket, and that we'd be expected to answer our boss's urgent messages over breakfast or while watching *The Tonight Show*.

But all that lies unimagined as Mazeroski careens counterclockwise through the late-afternoon sun, his ball clearing the fence of Forbes's notoriously spacious outfield lawn, coming to rest somewhere out there beyond the 406-foot sign, well to the right of the big Longines scoreboard. It lands in the soft green expanse of Schenley Park, settling immediately at a treasured spot in baseball lore. The Pirates, having vanquished the mighty Yankees, are champions, victors in a series so screwy that the MVP will be awarded to Bobby Richardson, the losing side's second baseman.

This moment will immortalize Bill Mazeroski, fuse him forever to his team's unlikely glory. It will also, in a few decades, factor into the conversation regarding his enshrinement in the Hall of Fame. He'll be elected in 2001 after languishing on the ballot for ten years of eligibility, his case taken up by the veterans committee. It will be true that his career tallies lack garish offensive numbers. Known as the Glove, his defence has always done the heavy work of buttressing his everyday reputation. But it will also remain true that most of us will know his name for this one very famous swing of the bat, and the swing will conduct attention like a lightning rod to his admirable steadiness.

The issue might be more semantic than statistical, and have less to do with Mazeroski's specific numbers and more with the definition of a Hall of Fame. The phrase—*The Hall of Fame*—and its vowelishness, its trim syllabic profile, is more pleasing than, say, Hall of Accomplishment or Hall of Recognition. It's also possible that "fame" bore different connotations in the mid-1930s, when the plan was hatched to erect a temple to baseball's greats in the game's mythical birthplace. Because if pure celebrity were the measure, Mazeroski's Yankees-killing dinger would be enough.

But then, if celebrity were the sole measure of Hall worthiness, José Canseco would unambiguously merit a plaque, as would Mark McGwire. Instead, it's sustained excellence that tips the scale in favour of enshrinement. The Glove put in seventeen seasons in the bigs, every one of them as a Pirate. For twelve straight campaigns—from 1957, his second year, to 1968—he played a minimum of 130 games. Mazeroski even managed to play 163 games in 1967. He embodied everydayness. Among his peers, his name was synonymous with durability, capability, professionalism—with showing up to work. His most well-known day at the office was October 13, 1960, but it was also just one of 2,175 days in which he turned in stellar defence and solid hitting.

He put in most of his work at 230 South Bouquet Street, a plot that Pirates owner Barney Dreyfuss purchased in 1908 with the support of Andrew Carnegie. The Schenley land had been a farm, then a park on the city's outskirts, and is today an arena of higher learning. And for a time, one of the most idyllic ballparks in history was situated on its northwest edge.

A constitutional weakness for nostalgia moves me to linger, forgive me, in the photos and paintings of Forbes Field. It was the embodiment of what architectural critic Paul Goldberger identifies as the essence of the ballpark: "the two sides of the American character—the Jeffersonian impulse toward open space and rural expanse, and the Hamiltonian belief in the city and in industrial infrastructure." Forbes Field, so perfectly situated on its very particular plot of land, arranged a rural idyll amid the urban grid, a green respite from the smog and tumult of Pittsburgh's twentieth-century cauldron of industry. Forbes Field hosted its inaugural game in June 1909; it was among the first of the steel and concrete "classic" American ballparks, following Philadelphia's Shibe Park by a few months, and preceding by a year the White Sox's Comiskey Park. These stadiums, replacing the oft-burned wooden grandstands of the previous century, lasted most of the twentieth century and are what a lot of us still picture when we close our eyes and think of a ballpark.

Forbes Field's outfield wall of red brick was overgrown with greenery and opened onto the landscaped beauty of Schenley Park. The stadium's interior surfaces were painted hunter green and were free of ads. For most of Forbes's life, its third-base stands were shadowed by the University of Pittsburgh's forty-two-storey limestone Gothic revival Cathedral of Learning. The whole scene is close to what an AI image generator would spit out if you fed it Goldberger's formula. If Doc Brown showed up in his DeLorean and offered me an afternoon anywhere, anytime, it would be hard to beat the afternoon of Game Seven of the 1960 World Series, sitting in box seats, watching Clemente patrol right and Maz manning second, inching toward his date with destiny.

The euphoria occasioned by that homer, and all those beautiful afternoons in Schenley Park, didn't prevent Pittsburgh from having a rough go of it in the ensuing couple of decades. The 1960s were great civically, with a wave of prosperity, though the Pirates floundered, failing to finish higher than third. The Bucs had to wait until 1971 to win another pennant, when they played in that first Series night game. They won again in '79, as the city saw its jobs begin to disappear. Industry gradually abandoned American urban centres, leaving Pittsburgh with a wealth of post-industrial waste, including a large collection of Superfund sites. In the early 1980s, the local unemployment rate reached 18.2 percent and the population severely declined. Maz might not recognize the place: Pittsburgh blighted, day baseball a rarity, and Forbes Field bulldozed. The future arrived, and it was bleak and unflatteringly lit.

But I've digressed—day baseball encourages daydreaming. And day baseball *isn't* dead; in 2024, teams were scheduled to play about twenty-one weekday games on average, and postseason baseball is partially daylit by necessity in each round preceding the World Series. The postseason has expanded from one to four rounds, and each game requires space on the broadcast/streaming schedule in order to maximize advertising impressions.

During the regular season, it's common for getaway day—the end of a mid-week series—to fall on a Wednesday or Thursday, giving the visitors a little more time to decamp and the home team extra hours to pack up before lighting out on a road trip. I've attended several such businessperson's specials at the Rogers Centre in the last few years. In Toronto, they're usually Thursdays, and while fewer working folks are slipping out of the office to attend, the games are full of school kids or day-campers, clumps of children in matching T-shirts occupying whole sections in the upper deck, weary counsellors ferrying an unending stream of them down to the upper concourse to visit the washroom. When the camera finds them and they appear on the videoboard, these children scream and bounce, clap and dance. Meanwhile, down below, the expensive seats are half-empty or worse, but temptingly bathed in Technicolor sunshine that begs to be soaked in.

After the last out, you can stroll in natural light to Union Station to catch your train, or grab some supper downtown. It's nice to get in nine innings before dinner. The schedule makers continue to tuck these little gems into their spreadsheets, and I happily search them out when the full season calendar is released.

On getaway days, the vibe around the park is laid back and a bit conspiratorial—we revel in having managed to steal an afternoon, whether in person or watching at home. But for the players, I imagine it tastes of the workday, their labours performed under the sun, an honest job to be done. Fields to be tilled, runs to be scored. It always feels to me like the embodiment of legendary Orioles manager Earl Weaver's words—"We do this every day"—with emphasis on "day."

As the season ages into October and November, the days shorten, clipping the daylight, pushing into the darkest hours those final outs. Try to imagine Maz's coup de grâce occurring after dark, the ball arcing against an inky black sky before disappearing into the gloom, the moment's author at the centre of a shooting star, his shadow thrown in eight different directions, uniform harshly white in the glare of the stadium's lamps. Still beautiful, I suppose, but not the same. And that feeling—of witnessing something so important that bosses gave their assent to those asking for the afternoon off—noticeably lacking.

It likely won't surprise you to learn that I'm in the category of people who'll stay up to watch the final inning of each World Series game no matter what. I'm doing the best I can with what we're given, I guess, and I'm worried I'll miss something amazing—like Maz's shot, or Kirk Gibson's, or Joe Carter's. I'm invariably watching alone; everyone else under our roof is in bed. And when the final out is recorded, I'm already standing, the remote in my hand, ready to shut off the TV and rush to join them, asleep before my head hits the pillow. At the breakfast table, I regale everyone with the highlights, pull my phone from my pocket and call up short videos of a big punchout or a bases-clearing double.

And then the kids are off to school and the whole day spreads out before me, ready to be used productively, a stark white page unblemished by anything as frivolous as a baseball game. By early afternoon I'm no longer of much use, dead tired from having stayed up, and a bit dismayed at the prospect of staying up late again to watch the next contest.

But Mazeroski took the field over two thousand times—surely I can stick it out to watch one more game. This, after all, is why I show up for baseball, year after year: its regularity, how it touches the vast majority of days from thaw to first frost. Workday, weeknight, weekend: there, dependably, like Maz.

LAKESHORE EAST

On work freely given and the places we find ourselves

We found a spot in the Oshawa park-and-ride lot. It turned out to be the only miracle we witnessed that particular Thursday. I never get a spot there, but Dad, driving his hybrid Hyundai Tucson, struck gold. The westbound train to Toronto's Union Station was waiting with doors open, so we hopped aboard, climbed up to the second deck, and shortly after found ourselves underway, skirting the lake's rim. We progressed through Whitby, Ajax, and Pickering. Past the St. Marys Cement plant, the Darlington Nuclear Generating Station, the Oshawa GM Assembly Plant, the Pickering Nuclear Generating Station, past various packaging operations and manufacturing concerns, past the GO Rail locomotive shop, distribution centres, shipping hubs.

To the south, over the water, the horizon was indistinct, awash in a beautiful summer haze, while in the foreground people who by good fortune or bad found themselves unscheduled on this early August weekday were engaged in an almost Victorian leisure-taking. Through the window of the train, the greens appeared too green, and the blues looked to have been infused with some rare metallic element that rendered them ultrablue. We sat side by side, my father and I, and talked about trains, played *Immaculate Grid* on my phone, and double-checked our tickets to that afternoon's game: Blue Jays and Orioles, a 3:07 p.m. start, decent seats, my birthday gift to Dad.

The world slid steadily by: industry and suburb, construction, highway, parks, soccer fields, ball diamonds. These eastern outposts of the Greater Toronto Area began, in most cases, as small, distinct towns, but in time, as the big city sprawled out, were subsumed, until they resembled a Cheever-esque suburban landscape of swimming pools and commuter trains, their inhabitants largely employed somewhere in the gleaming metropolis, forever.

But something changed. The economy diversified and demographics shifted. Strip malls sprouted. Post-industrial disruption, immigration, changing family units, underfunded infrastructure, asymmetrical growth, cycles of retrenchment, and calamity (financial, pathogenic) all changed these and uncountable similar communities. Because of, or despite, all this, people formed relationships to these outposts, this area—Lakeshore East, as GO Transit refers to the ground it covers—making them places in and of themselves, where people live, work, and play.

My relationship to these places is unquestionably shaped by work. The same is true for the places where I grew up, the places my father grew up. My father's parents fled the Second World War, leaving their small English town and landing in Hamilton, Ontario, where my grandfather's experience as a tool and die maker got him hired by Westinghouse Electric Corporation. And that's where my father grew up, at the western end of the Golden Horseshoe where Lake Ontario terminates. Dad went to Royal Military College in Kingston, at the eastern end of the lake. He spent nearly thirty years in the Royal

Canadian Navy, which brought our family to Ottawa, Halifax, and back to Ottawa. That's where I spent most of my childhood and young adult life. Then Christie's job with the provincial government took us to Kemptville, Ontario, and then to Peterborough, where our kids have grown up. My folks stayed in their house in Ottawa until Mom's health deteriorated, at which point they moved to Peterborough to be closer to me. Mom died a few years ago, but Dad has stayed nearby, meaning Peterborough is his part of the world now too, however improbably.

So here we are, three generations of people whose lives have been fixed geographically, and given their particular character, by patterns of economic migration and settlement following broad lines of work.

Peterborough isn't (yet?) contiguous to the GTA—it rests east and north, and is still separated physically by undeveloped land, and philosophically by its association with cottage country and lack of direct rail link to downtown Toronto. My spatial relationship to Toronto has been consistent my entire life; I've never lived west of the city. When entering the Big Smoke to take in a Blue Jays game—to see Dave Stieb or Carlos Delgado or Vlad Guerrero Jr.—my approach has always been from the east, meaning the trip has always brought me through Oshawa, Whitby, Ajax, Pickering.

The communities Dad and I glimpsed from the window of that air-conditioned commuter train have long presaged baseball for me. And as my kids have begun to play competitive sports, this part of the world—the vast and variated area east and north of Toronto—has been the setting for their athletic development, the names of various municipalities stitched or screened across the uniforms of the teams they play.

Soccer was first. Adelaide began as a halfback who played tenacious defence, and was dependable for strong, accurate throw-ins, though she occasionally played forward too. From May through October, the Peterborough City Soccer Association team played home games at Eastgate Memorial Park in Peterborough and road games in Oshawa, Darlington, North York, Lindsay, Cavan, Uxbridge. Then she fell in love with volleyball, and her brothers, given some exposure to it, fell in love too. Club volleyball, school volleyball, beach volleyball camp, and a Saturday night recreational volleyball league. Tournaments in school gyms, community centres, and convention halls.

And baseball. Both boys suited up and took to fields in Orono, Ajax, Pickering, Oshawa, Warkworth, Wellington, Bowmanville. Tournaments in London, Orillia, Brockville. At Durham College.

Once or twice a week I'd drive the big roads—the 401, the 407, the 412—and the smaller ones until we arrived at the right ball field, usually a lone diamond or a clover-shaped complex. I'd release my kid to the coaches' care and then find a suitable spot along a baseline, erect a folding chair, and sit and wait for the game to start.

Eventually—just ahead of the first year that our thirteen-year-old twin sons would be teammates—their head coach, Dave, emailed to ask if I'd consider joining as an assistant coach. "It was only a matter of time," Christie said. Meaning not that my vast experience and great expertise were at last being recognized with the invitation, but rather that within the network of care provided by kids' sports, it'll eventually be your turn to step up and volunteer for something.

I spent that winter attending clinics and getting the requisite certification, and began helping with indoor workouts while there was still snow on the ground. The team practised at a hardware store and lumber yard that'd been converted into a fitness centre. Throwing, fielding, and tee work, progressing to live hitting, first from coaches' pitches and then from the two pitching machines available to us.

By May we were outdoors, the fields at last snowless and dry if not yet green. I took up my post in the third-base coaching box, counselling baserunners who possessed a jackrabbit's urge to bolt, telling them, "We don't want to run ourselves out of the inning." Reminding them how many outs there are, and how that determines what they do on a ball in play.

I helped to plan and run practices, to cajole the boys through pregame warm-ups, and to act as a catch partner or emergency bullpen catcher when the numbers required it. I offered counsel on lineup decisions. I cheered from the dugout when we were on defence, and when hitting I signalled to runners when to steal and when to stay. I exercised my judgment on passed balls, saying, "No, no, no," when the ball remained close to the catcher, or, "Yes, yes, go!" when it rolled to the backstop and the pitcher was slow to cover the plate. Win or lose, I reminded the boys to hustle down the baseline when the handshakes were done, to take a knee in the outfield grass and listen to the head coach as he delivered postgame remarks. If invited, I offered a few words of my own and then slapped high-fives as the players drifted off with parents and guardians toward parked cars and drives home. I carted buckets of balls, hitting nets, bags of equipment to the head coach's truck. I stood in gravel lots in hot sun or beneath LED lamps in the paved and landscaped outer reaches of lavish new community athletic facilities and chatted with the other coaches. We talked about what we saw and what we might do different, about the kid who surprised us or the kid whose head didn't seem to be in it these days. We talked about how good the cold beer would taste when we finally made it home.

My commitment totalled a dozen or fifteen hours a week at the height of summer, more on tournament weekends, and less in the offseason when we might have had two hours of training in an inflatable dome on Saturday mornings and another couple hours of hitting practice in the batting cages at a CrossFit facility. Always there were emails bouncing around about new drills we might try or thoughts on a kid who might be a candidate to switch positions.

I was a small cog in the great machine. Others, whether coaches or administrators, team managers, or families, did far, far more. Some volunteered to coordinate walk-up music, recording intros, mixing songs, and running it all through an app on a phone connected to a wireless speaker positioned behind the backstop. Others pitched in to do a bit of supplemental groundskeeping, to set up shade tents, organize fundraisers, book hotels, wash uniforms, keep growing thirteen-year-olds fed, and get them to practice and games on time. For their heroic toil, these volunteers were rewarded with the opportunity to shiver through chilly night games in May, huddle beneath umbrellas or canopies in June downpours, or swelter through afternoon doubleheaders in July.

A considerable amount of effort, the co-operation of a good many people, goes into seven innings of youth baseball. All of it is a kind of work, but it is work freely given, the returns intangible but every bit real.

★★★

As the kids grew older, Christie and I found ourselves on the go twelve months of the year, giving somebody a ride somewhere five or six days a week. Practice, game, tournament. Volleyball, soccer, badminton, tennis, basketball, baseball. One of my sons, Cormac, began playing competitive ultimate frisbee.

Our passengers read, snacked, pored over portable game consoles and phones, and placed muddy cleats on the dashboard and seatbacks while lacing up. They forgot essential pieces of equipment, they spilled colourful sports drinks. They asked if they had to go to practice, to which we reminded them: We don't force you to sign up, but once you've signed up, we expect you'll stand by the commitment. When the season's done, if you want to quit, you can quit.

Once we got to where we were going—Belleville? Barrie?—we chatted with the other parents, made impromptu equipment repairs, and attempted to herd loud assemblies of overstimulated kids out of hotel hallways. We planned and registered and paid.

We bought new cleats, new court shoes, new knee pads, new gloves, bats, tapes, wraps. We washed and repaired and packed uniforms. We downloaded new apps, logged attendance, replied to emails, organized fundraising. We drove some more. We consoled and bolstered, we listened. We worried and feared. We bit our tongues.

Once the practice or game or tournament was over, we reversed course and motored back toward Peterborough along sodium-lit 400-series highways, or down quiet backroads, through fields swallowed by borderless dark, stopping at distant floodlit waystations for food and gas before we continued home.

And when it seemed like too much, Christie and I would remind each other that these years would be over too quickly.

That we'd miss all of them when they were gone, and we'd likely wonder what to do with so much free time to ourselves.

***

The train pulled into Union Station on time. Dad and I walked west with the thickening masses toward the Dome and scanned in at the left-field gate. It was all teed up to be a perfect afternoon. The sun beat full bore down on us, the roof open, the CN Tower stretching up toward a perfect blue sky.

We had great seats, just a few rows up from field level, near the corner in left. We were close enough to see the grimace on left fielder Daulton Varsho's face when he charged a skipping liner by Adley Rutschman with the bases loaded in the second inning and launched a rocket toward home to nail Austin Hays for the third out.

"Looks like everybody's working from home today," said a beer vendor, who was doing brisk business in the heat. More than forty-two thousand had wandered into the Dome this Thursday afternoon, deferring their responsibilities.

Toronto's starter Kevin Gausman's vaunted splitter wasn't having its intended effect; he threw it consistently low, and the Orioles exercised patience, laying off it, getting ahead in counts, forcing him to throw strikes, pitches they could hit. Baltimore first sacker Ryan Mountcastle, who always seems to kill the Jays, was 4-for-4 on the afternoon with two runs scored and an RBI. The Blue Jays managed a run off Jack Flaherty in the sixth but ended the frame with the bases loaded.

Final: 6–1 for the bad guys.

In the warm evening, Dad and I made our way back toward Union. We stopped for dinner to let the postgame train crowd thin, then ducked into the station, found our platform, and hopped aboard the Lakeshore East train, taking seats up top across from a man in red suspenders who'd slid his stockinged feet out of his running shoes. Seeing our Jays caps, he said, "Boy, they really stunk it up today, huh?"

His name was Ted, also from Peterborough, and he'd been at the game too. Ted was a bus driver for the local transit commission, the sort of old-stock Ontarian who'd lived in our city when it was a small town. He'd spent years, he said, refereeing hockey and umpiring baseball in Peterborough. Overfull of what he considered common sense, he told us the problem with youth hockey now was that we'd taken all the hitting out of the game. "So now they don't know how to *get* hit," he said.

And though I didn't agree with him, it bore facing that Ted and I—and my father, for that matter—were residents of the same town, both implicated in the life of that place in a variety of ways. When I think of community, it seems to me that what we mean, in large measure, is us: Ted and I, and my dad, the kids we coach and raise. That's not all of it, I know, but those threads are part of the weave that forms our local fabric.

Once at the train's terminus in Oshawa, Ted discovered that his bus back to Peterborough didn't leave for an hour, so Dad offered him a ride. We weren't on the road long—Dad driving, me riding shotgun, Ted in the middle of the back seat—before the skies opened, great gushing sheets occasionally lit by the white lamp of lightning.

Our paths are aleatoric, even accidental, and the brain's desire for narrative reorders events in retrospect to suggest the inevitability of our arrival and occupation in a given place. Connections can help make such arrangements less happenstantial, and so more solid, and I don't think there are better civic connections to be made than putting your kids on a local team. That's how root memories are formed for all concerned: your kids sweating and striving, succeeding and failing alongside your neighbours' children, whether they're long-time residents or newly landed citizens who blink, and, bewildered, whisper to themselves, "How did I get here?" just as I did and indeed still do.

The answer, often, is that work brought you to where you are, and by work will you make it your home.

SHUCKS AND THE BABE

On second thoughts, debuts, summer jobs, and striking out Babe Ruth

Hubert Shelby "Shucks" Pruett was born on September 1, 1900, in Malden, Missouri, down near the boot heel, as some folks call the protuberance that juts into Arkansas. Malden is closer to Memphis than St. Louis and, as Hub's grandson, Jamie Pruett, told me in 2023, it's "a nothing little part of Missouri."

If you go digging into Hub Pruett's biography, you'll come across a few different places identified as his birthplace, including Louisville, Kentucky, and Higginsville, Missouri, which is over toward Kansas City. But census records show he was from Malden.

Hub's father, Shelby Pruett, died in an accident when Shucks was only four years old. Family lore holds that Shelby was in a carriage that overturned. Shucks's mother had a hard life following her husband's death. "I think they moved in with grandparents," said Jamie, "her parents. We don't have a lot of that story." We do know that Hub attended high school in Dexter, which was about seventeen miles due north of Malden. When he graduated, the family managed to scrape together enough to send him to the University of Missouri, where he played for the Tigers. And we know that's where Cardinals scout Charley Barrett saw him. Shucks made the trip to St. Louis, encountered Bob Quinn, worked out for the Browns' manager, and was offered a contract—which Pruett declined.

Instead, he went back to school to continue his studies. In spring 1921, Pruett again suited up for the University of Missouri Tigers. Early that season, the team travelled to St. Louis to play Washington University. Now that he was securely on their radar, the Browns sent scout Pat Monahan to offer Pruett a chance to reconsider. This time Shucks signed.

When Shucks reported to the Browns, his throwing arm was in a sling. Possibly this was just a bit of bad timing, or maybe it would prove a sign of things to come. Pruett was sent down to the Tulsa Oilers of the Western League, where he totalled 135 innings of work and gave up an even 100 runs. He won four games and lost seven.

He'd hardly set the world on fire, but he'd done enough to get noticed. By the following spring, he was wearing a big-league uniform because the Browns—like every baseball team since the advent of overhand pitching—decided they couldn't have too many lefty hurlers.

In 1922, everything came together for the Browns.

Manager Lee Fohl had replaced Jimmy Burke at the helm in 1921 after steering Cleveland for parts of five seasons.

Manning first, George Sisler had a season for the ages, batting .420, totalling 246 hits (eleven shy of his 1920 total, a record for hits in a season that stood for eighty-four years, until Ichiro broke it). He also stole fifty-one bases. Along the way, he managed a forty-one-game hitting streak. This was all good, in modern parlance, for a 1.061 OPS. For his troubles, Sisler was handed the first American League MVP award.

Outfielder Ken Williams, a lefty-hitting Oregonian, chipped in thirty-nine homers and 155 RBIs, both representing league-best numbers in the AL that year. He also stole thirty-nine bases (and was caught twenty times, suggesting that Fohl and the Browns' strategists weren't big on advanced analytics), making him history's first thirty–thirty man.

Veteran catcher Hank Severeid was a sturdy backstop and a strong hitter who contributed a .321 average and seventy-eight RBIs in 1922. Second baseman Marty McManus and outfielder Baby Doll Jacobson both hit over .300 and added more than one hundred RBIs each.

The pitching was good too. The staff was anchored by the once-and-future Yankee Urban Shocker, who, because I was born in Canada's capital, I'm duty bound to mention spent two seasons with the Ottawa Senators of the Class B Canadian League, winning championships in both. Shocker had gone 27–12 for the Browns in 1921, and followed that up with a 24–17 record in '22. Behind him were Elam Vangilder, Dixie Davis, Ray Kolp, and Rasty Wright, along with a handful of capable relievers. The St. Louis hurlers put together a team ERA of 3.38, the lowest in the American League.

Fuelled by all that, the Brownies spent most of the summer neck and neck with the Yankees atop the American League.

It also helped that Babe Ruth had gotten himself into a little trouble. The Yankees lost the 1921 World Series to the Giants, and Ruth was banged up in the process, injuring an arm and leg. After the Series, Ruth and some other Yankees engaged in a little light barnstorming, contravening a rule that stated players from pennant-winning teams were barred from post-Series tours. Commissioner Landis suspended Ruth and fellow Yank Bob Meusel for the first six weeks of the 1922 season and fined them their championship shares.

The Babe returned to the lineup on May 20, and he struggled. By May 25, batting a frustrating .136, Ruth argued an umpire's out call, threw dirt in the arbiter's face, and, after being tossed, he challenged fans to a fight. He was fined again and stripped of the team captaincy. Ruth was suspended once more in June when he got into an altercation with umpire Bill Dineen.

In all, Ruth played only 110 games that season, while Ken Williams was a constant in the Browns' lineup that year, playing in all but one game. That almost certainly helped Williams claim the AL home-run title, besting the Babe by four. (Rogers Hornsby walloped forty-two homers for the NL's Cardinals to lead all of baseball.)

Ruth would end the season with disappointing totals (35 HR, 96 RBIs, 94 runs scored). While his pure performance represented a dip from his absurdly brilliant 1921 season, his '22 AL-best OPS (1.106) tells us he was still swinging the bat better than just about anyone else on the planet.

One area in which he would struggle became apparent just a couple of days into his truncated '22 season, when Hub Pruett and the Browns visited the Yankees at the Polo Grounds in Upper Manhattan on May 22.

★★★

Shucks saw no game action for the first couple weeks of the 1922 season. He finally made his major-league debut on April 26 at Sportsman's Park, when he held the Tigers scoreless in the top of the ninth inning in an eventual 2–0 loss to Detroit. He next appeared on May 8 in Washington when he entered in relief of Dave Danforth, down two runs in the fourth inning. Hub struck out the Senators' Bucky Harris before getting a bit shaky, walking the next two batters, then retiring Joe Judge on a fielder's choice before allowing Sam Rice to score on a wild pitch. He finished the frame by striking out Frank Bower. In all, Hub pitched four innings, giving up that one run but otherwise avoiding damage, and the Browns scored twice in the seventh and twice more in the ninth for a comeback win.

Pruett's next outing was a start in that same series on May 11. Rewarding Hub's "meritorious relief service" in the earlier game, manager Fohl went with the southpaw in the finale. Shucks pitched into the fifth and though he was a little wild—surrendering five bases on balls—he earned the win in a 5–3 Browns victory.

Hub did an inning of mop-up duty against the A's in a lopsided defeat on May 15 and then sat for a week. When he was next summoned, the Browns were visiting the Yankees at the Polo Grounds. With the game tied at three, New York had a runner on first in the bottom of the ninth inning. Pruett got Elmer Miller to pop out to the first baseman and Aaron Ward to line out to third to end the inning.

In the bottom of the tenth, with the score still knotted, Ruth strode to the plate.

To this point—the tenth inning of this game against the Browns on May 22, 1922—Babe Ruth had 163 career home runs, the most recent of which had come in the eighth inning off Vangilder. It's impossible to overstate the monumental shift in baseball that Ruth oversaw. He batted third that afternoon, ahead of the cleanup man, Frank "Home Run" Baker, who was in the final season of a thirteen-year Hall of Fame career. Baker was the pre-eminent slugger of the Deadball Era. He earned his nickname by hitting two big shots against the Giants in the

1911 World Series, and led or co-led the American League in home runs every year from 1911 to 1914.

Home Run Baker never hit more than twelve round-trippers in a season.

The policy of the day had been to use a single ball for an entire game, where possible, which resulted in softened, misshapen, and darkened balls. Generally, even if you got a good swing on a ball it wasn't going to go very far. It's likely that players modelled their hitting styles in recognition of that fact; small ball ruled the day. But rule changes before the 1920 season stipulated that umpires should use their discretion to replace marred baseballs with fresh ones, which would be whiter, and so easier to see, and firmer, resulting in hits that travelled farther.

And then in August 1920, at the Polo Grounds, Cleveland shortstop Ray Chapman failed to duck a Carl Mays fastball and took the pitch to the head, succumbing to the injury the next morning at St. Lawrence Hospital in the Bronx. It was said that Chapman's fatal beaning was accidental on Mays's part, the result of a grey afternoon inching toward twilight, and a discoloured ball. Witnesses claimed it appeared that Chapman never even saw the pitch. In the wake of the tragedy, the rule regarding new balls was to be enforced even more rigorously.

Enter Ruth. In 1920, playing under the new rule, and in his first season as a Yankee, he hit fifty-four home runs. The following season he hit fifty-nine. His raw power, when coupled with the sudden changes to the game and the construction of smaller ballparks, ushered in a new era of baseball, one characterized by offence.

Ruth was an imposing figure, at six feet, two inches tall, and officially listed at 215 pounds, but let's take that as the baseline. By 1922, the trappings of legend had begun to accumulate around him. He'd already achieved a level of fame virtually unknown in the history of sports, his ascent coinciding with the rise of American popular media. He was well on his way to becoming the most famous man in the world.

And the Babe was digging in to face Pruett, a small and delicate-looking rookie pitcher listed at five feet ten, inches tall and 165 pounds, in the tenth inning of a tie ballgame.

"When I went out to the mound, I didn't know who he was," Pruett said years later. "I was just a country boy. Ruth was just another hitter to me. All I knew was that he was a left-handed hitter, and I didn't have much trouble with left-handers."

Hub got ahead of Ruth, a ball and two strikes.

Shucks may not have been an imposing figure. But he had a devastating pitch in his arsenal.

Ruth fouled one off. Then, according to Pruett, he unleashed the fadeaway.

★★★

Somewhere along the way, prior to his college days, Hub Pruett encountered Barney Pelty.

Pelty was a righty curveball specialist. He bounced around a bit before catching on with the Browns. His *Sporting News* card summarizes his movements thusly: "Nashville, 1902 as catcher-jumped club and signed with independent Cairo, Ill. club, 1902. Cedar Rapids, 1903. Sold to St. Louis AL Aug. 1903," and there follows a string of years all the way up to 1912. Pelty finished up his major-league career with the Senators in 1913. Along the way, he showed flashes of brilliance: On July 4, 1906, he took a no-hitter into the ninth against the White Sox (his catcher: Branch Rickey) before giving up a ground ball that his inexperienced, fill-in shortstop couldn't handle. And on April 23, 1909, he threw a gutsy complete game to beat Cy Young and the Cleveland Naps 3–1.

Pelty was from Farmington, Missouri, about sixty-five or seventy miles south of St. Louis, and by all accounts that's where his post-baseball life was centred. In Farmington, Pelty coached high school sports, ran a store, dabbled in local politics, and worked as a food inspector and a construction foreman.

When Hub was a boy, the greatest pitcher of the day was the Giants' Christy Mathewson. Matty's favourite and best pitch was what he called a fadeaway. Shucks wanted to throw it too. We'd be more likely to recognize the fadeaway as a screwball, a pitch that breaks opposite to a slider or curveball, which is to say out and away from the pitcher's hand instead of across his body. Pruett approached Pelty and, in his own words, "asked him if I could learn the fadeaway even though I was a left-hander. Barney said he would coach me and pretty soon I was throwing it pretty well."

"By the time I was pitching for the varsity at the University of Missouri," Pruett later told *The Sporting News*, "the opposing hitters weren't getting a foul off the fadeaway. I threw the fadeaway three ways. Thrown overhand, it acted somewhat like a slider—it moved out. Underhand [by which I take him to mean sidearm], the ball nose-dived—this was my big strikeout pitch. I also threw it with a three-quarter motion. Any way I threw it, the ball would break sharply away from a right-handed batter, break into a left-handed hitter."

There weren't many pitches Ruth couldn't handle, but he couldn't handle that one.

Which is why the Babe went down swinging on his first meeting with Pruett.

★★★

That might be enough for most of us, to be able to say, "I struck out Babe Ruth once." Reputations are built on less. But Shucks began to make a habit of it.

They next faced each other on June 12, when Hub was again given the start. He struck Ruth out in the first, walked him in the fourth, struck him out in the sixth, and again in the eighth.

The press loved it. They called Shucks a "puny collegian," told of how he was "poison to Ruth."

On July 12, the Browns and the Yankees met again. Pruett made the start, inducing the Babe to ground out to first in the inaugural frame, strikeout swinging in the third, strikeout looking in the fifth, and strikeout swinging in the sixth.

On August 25, Hub came in for two innings of relief work, inserted with the bases loaded and none out, with Ruth coming to bat. Hub fanned the Babe once more.

Over a twenty-two-year career comprising 10,628 plate appearances, Ruth struck out a total of 1,330 times, or about once every eight times he strode up to bat. (For comparison, through the first eight seasons of his career, Aaron Judge struck out about once every three and a half plate appearances.) But in their first eleven meetings, this kid named Pruett had struck out the fearsome Ruth eight times, to go with two walks and a groundout.

Shucks owned the Babe.

★★★

They called it the Little World Series: The Yankees held a slender half-game lead over the Browns, and it was widely understood that this three-game series in mid-September would all but determine the American League pennant.

Sisler had hit in thirty-nine straight games. Shocker had already won twenty-three. Ken Williams had thirty-seven home runs to date. The Browns' staff led the league in ERA and strikeouts.

The Yankees were riding great pitching too, from Bullet Joe Bush, Bob Shawkey, Waite Hoyte, Sad Sam Jones, and Carl Mays, with relief help from George Murray. Ruth had thirty-two dingers, and the rest of the lineup was hitting too—first baseman Wally Pipp was having an outstanding year, as was catcher Wally Schang. Big Bob Meusel added sixteen homers of his own to Ruth's gaudy total.

But the Browns had Shucks.

Fans in St. Louis were worked up. In the bottom of the ninth of the first game on Saturday afternoon, with New York up 2–1, things got heated.

The Yankees' centre fielder was Whitey Witt. His real name was Ladislaw Waldemar Wittkowski, but Connie Mack of the Philadelphia A's truncated it early on in Wittkowski's career: "Mack didn't want to write Wittkowski on the batting card every day," said the outfielder, "so he changed my name to Witt. Then, because I had blond hair, he called me Whitey."

Browns fans hissed and jeered, and Witt was struck in the head by a bottle thrown from the stands. He fell unconscious, and spectators, sensing imminent pandemonium, edged onto the field. Several Yankees sprung from the dugout, ready to defend their wounded comrade. Police managed to stave off a potential riot and the game resumed, though the wind was out of the Browns' sails. Elmer Smith replaced Witt, and with one out, Sisler, who'd doubled in the fourth to extend his hitting streak to forty games, attempted to bunt his way on. Shawkey fielded the ball and retired Sisler at first. Then Ken Williams flied out to end the game. Shocker had gone the distance and pitched well, so Pruett hadn't been required. Shawkey had just pitched better.

Sunday's game featured Waite Hoyt on the mound for New York. The Schoolboy had signed his first pro contract at the age of fifteen with the New York Giants, but had gone on an extended sojourn through the minors before finally making his big-league debut at eighteen. Just a year older than Shucks, Hoyt had appeared in seventy-nine games before Pruett's career even began. He'd play twenty-one years for seven different organizations, en route to 237 wins and a plaque in the Hall of Fame.

Fohl countered with Pruett, starting his eighth game of the season, his thirty-sixth appearance overall. Hub struck out Witt and Joe Dugan to start the contest, then walked Ruth. He got lucky when Wally Pipp tried to stretch a single and was put out at second, stranding the Babe at third.

The Bambino led off the fourth inning. Shucks struck him out on four pitches.

It remained a scoreless game until the sixth, when, with two out and nobody on, Ruth again swaggered to the dish. With the count at 2–2, Hub reared and delivered.

Sportsman's Park had a cavernous centre field, probably measuring about 445 feet in 1922, and a fairly spacious lawn in left. Right field was small, just 315 feet, necessitated by the presence of North Grand Boulevard, which squeezed the ground's footprint uncomfortably. The wall out there stood a dozen feet high, and by 1929 it was topped by a screen that effectively tripled its height. But that screen wasn't present in 1922, and the tight dimension to his pull side almost certainly helped Williams's power numbers—just as Yankee Stadium, which would open in 1923, would be tailor-cut to Ruth's swing.

On this occasion, on this pitch, Babe seemed to approve of Sportsman's Park: he deposited the offering over the wall in right. Yankees 1, Browns 0, and Ruth's blanking at Hub's hand ended. But the Browns weren't quite sunk. In the bottom of the inning, third baseman Eddie Foster walked and Sisler singled him over to second, extending his hitting streak to forty-one games in the process. Ken Williams drove in Foster, and Severeid knocked in Sisler and Williams. In the eighth, Williams homered to right with Sisler on base to make the score 5–1.

Pruett, meanwhile, was cruising, with Ruth's homer the only hiccup. The Yankees had a little something going in the top of the ninth with Shucks still pitching, but things ended on a nifty double play when Hub struck out Wally Schang, and Severeid nailed Pipp trying to work his way into scoring position by larcenous means.

While Ruth had to a degree solved Pruett, at least on this afternoon, Hub's line was impressive: one run on five hits, five strikeouts and a single walk. With the victory, the Browns were back to within a half game of New York, with one more head-to-head matchup the following afternoon.

★★★

The 1930s were hard on the Browns, as they were on just about everyone. Except for maybe the Cardinals, who won three pennants and two World Series in the Depression-blighted decade, stealing the hearts of St. Louis baseball fans in the process.

In 1935, the Browns drew a total of 80,922 fans, while the Cardinals, playing in the same ballpark, welcomed 506,084. The

Browns were last in the American League in attendance every year from 1926 to 1943.

The team was consistently bad, and fans stayed home in impressive numbers. A series of owners failed to invest in both Sportsman's Park, leading to its deterioration, and the team, leading to its poor performance. A glimmer of hope came during the war, when a ragtag team of draft-ineligible players took the Browns to an American League pennant and a spot in the 1944 World Series—against the Cardinals, who won in six games. Bill Veeck bought the team in 1951, but he couldn't turn them into a winner, and in 1953 the team was sold to a group of investors who moved them to Baltimore and renamed them the Orioles.

So 1922 really was the high-water mark for the Browns, arguably the afternoon when a rookie pitcher with a strange mastery over the Babe shut down the Yankees to pull St. Louis to within a half game of first. That was as close as they would ever get.

★★★

The day after Pruett's 5–1 win, Bullet Joe Bush took the mound for the Yankees and the Browns countered with Dixie Davis. Both righties pitched well, keeping the game scoreless until the fifth when Severeid cashed in Jacobson. McManus knocked in Ken Williams in the seventh to make it 2–0 St. Louis. The Yanks scored one in the eighth to make it 2–1.

Dixie Davis retook the hill in the ninth. He gave up a leadoff single to Wally Schang, who then scampered to second on a wild pitch. Lee Fohl turned to Shucks, who only the day before had thrown a full nine innings. Hub's balky arm was tired, and he wouldn't manage to record an out. Mike McNally laid down a bunt that Severeid couldn't field in time. Pruett then walked Everett Scott to load the bases.

Fohl had seen enough. He sized up his bullpen and opted for Shocker, calling the veteran in on less than a day's rest.

Hope flickered when Shocker got the first out on a force at the plate, but Witt, recovered from his bottle-beaning two days prior, singled to score McNally and Scott. Shocker finished the inning by getting Dugan to ground into a double play, 5–4–3.

Suddenly trailing 3–2, the Browns mustered nothing in the ninth. Sisler, Williams, and Jacobson went down in order. Pruett, whose runners Shocker had inherited, was stuck with the loss. In the span of twenty-four hours he'd gone from hero to heel, and the Browns slipped another game back. Within days they'd be four and a half behind with only a week left to play. The Browns ended up winning six of nine games down the homestretch after the Yankees series, but it wasn't enough. They finished the season exactly one game behind New York. The Browns' moment had passed them by.

But things still looked good for Hub Pruett. He was twenty-two years old, and, his last game against the Yankees notwithstanding, had displayed a rare ability to send Babe Ruth sulking back to the dugout. His arm was sore, but it had been a long season; who wasn't sore? Surely a long career in baseball was in the cards for Shucks.

"My early ambition was to be a doctor, and I never started to be a ball player," recalled Pruett, speaking to *The Sporting News*. "When I was pitching for the University of Missouri, it never occurred to me that my little curve could fool big league hitters. Then, when an offer came to play pro ball, I accepted with the idea of earning some money while working my way through medical school."

"He doesn't dissipate," the Dexter *Statesman* wrote of Hub on June 2, 1922. "He saves his money. He gets $3,000 for six months with the Browns [officially, his contract was for $2,500], and he salts down two out of every three to pay his way in the university in the winter."

Some students wait tables, or head north to plant trees, or work as camp counsellors. Hub's summer job included the opportunity to strike out Babe Ruth.

On September 27, Pruett left the Browns to resume his studies. He'd thrown 119.2 innings in his rookie year, and had the lowest opponent's batting average in the AL, at .235.

As recorded on his index card in *The Sporting News* collection, Hub would return the following summer to "St. Louis A.Lg." Based on his overall performance in 1922, including his mastery of Ruth, he'd get a bump in pay to $4,200. He had all winter to rest and rebuild his strength, and he'd made enough money to cover tuition.

Pruett was on his way as both a pitcher of elevated ability and as a doctor of medicine. Sooner or later, though, he was going to have to choose a specialization: Was he going to challenge hitters or treat patients?

THE BODY AND THE MACHINE

On Albert Pujols's longevity, degradation, and the worker's body as the means of production

We live in an entropic universe. The second law of thermodynamics states that everything tends toward disorder and that all systems progress from order to chaos. In other words, things fall apart.

This most certainly includes your body. I'm reminded of this every baseball practice, every time I throw a BP session or crouch to catch warm-up pitches. Disintegration is non-negotiable. It's the foundation of all creation. From nothing, to something, and on its way to nothing again.

This inescapable truth, as it concerns baseball, shapes all career arcs, from Shucks to Ruth to Jackie Robinson to Shohei Ohtani. It's often framed as a what-if: What if Mantle hadn't wrecked his knees? What if Koufax's arm had held together? How many homers would Griffey Jr. have hit if his legs remained healthy?

What if Albert Pujols's feet, right elbow, and left knee hadn't slowed him down?

★★★

My kids don't believe me when I tell them how good Pujols was. There are two things at play here. First, he was a quiet superstar. As his nickname, the Machine, suggests, Pujols was relentlessly consistent but not flashy. Second, my kids only knew him at the end of his career, when the game had caught up with his body and he was routinely at or near the very bottom of baseball in statistics like sprint speed. It was easy to see only the liability he'd become for the Angels, especially if all you'd known was slow Albert, a dead pull hitter in the heart of the defensive shift era.

So for them, and anyone who may have forgotten or missed those prime years, at his peak, Pujols was a three-time National League MVP, and he might have made it five had not his career coincided with Barry Bonds's most gonzo years. He also finished second in MVP voting twice—to Ryan Howard in 2006, and in 2010 to Joey Votto, who said he was "shocked" at the results.

At different times from 2001 until that 2010 campaign, the Cardinals' tall, barrel-chested first baseman achieved league-best numbers in runs, hits, doubles, home runs, average, RBIs, on base percentage, slugging, OPS, and total bases. He was the 2001 Rookie of the Year, an All-Star in nine of his first ten seasons, a six-time Silver Slugger, and won two Gold Gloves. There wasn't much Albert Pujols couldn't do on a baseball field.

He hit free agency after ten years of service in St. Louis. He was one of the best hitters the game had seen, thirty-one years old, and looking for some security. The Angels stepped up and offered him a ten-year, $240 million deal.

★★★

A non-controversial statement: baseball requires baseball players. Playing baseball constitutes labour. With the professionalization of the game, team owners became employers, paying ballplayers. We own your labour, said the owners, and because your labour cannot be performed without the instrument of your body, we effectively own that too.

Marx's definition of the means of production excludes the worker's body; the body is the source of labour, not an instrument. But whereas technological innovations can supplant labour (and in turn become the means of production), in the case of baseball and sport more generally, the body cannot be replaced by technological means (unless we're willing to cheer for machines, which, I mean, no thanks). The athlete's body is necessary to produce the good. So the ballplayer sells not only his labour but simultaneously the means of production to the contracting team.

Further, as Pujols and so many others so clearly demonstrate, the very production of the commodity or commodities ("entertainment"; "baseball") degrades the tools required to create them. "The act of production itself is thus in all its phases also an act of consumption," wrote Marx. As regards baseball, the longer and harder you play, the more damage done to the means of production.

When free agency became the norm in the late 1970s, owners begrudgingly allowed that baseball players are themselves tools, but the players ultimately own the instrument and lease it to contracting teams. Negotiating the terms of those contracts requires both parties to acknowledge the inevitable degradation of the tool while seeking different ends. Teams look to ensure they're paying for maximum performance, while a player hopes to leverage his instrument's prime years against job security (and continued earning) once the tool starts to break down.

Pujols is a prime illustration of this tension, not because the entropy of his body prevented him from having a great career, but because it prevented a great career from being among the absolute greatest careers ever to have been played. During the drawn-out end of his playing days, when the breakdown of the instrument was impossible to ignore, it became difficult for the Angels to give him playing time. And it was hard to justify parking a player earning $28 million a season on the bench.

If health were no concern, Pujols's name would be spoken in the same reverent tone as that of Mays or Aaron. He finished his career with 703 home runs—fourth all-time behind Ruth (714), Aaron (755), and Bonds (762), making him one of only four men to have hit 700 or more. If he'd played more than the 89 percent of games available to him, how many more might he have hit? How much higher on that list would he be?

Albert Pujols did just fine. He'll be a Hall of Famer once he's eligible in 2028, and he made north of $300 million in his career, exactly the sort of compensation his predecessors fought for. But his career probably would have been a whole lot shorter if the success he enjoyed in the first half of it hadn't granted him the right to negotiate for security in the back half. A couple of decades previous, the damage to his body by forces beyond his control would have had him wandering the figurative desert, stringing together one-year contracts until they dried up, preventing him from adding to his numbers. That, in turn, would have denied many of us the opportunity to watch a legend ply his trade—his skill galactic in scope, his aggregate accomplishments so astonishing you'd be forgiven for suspecting they were produced by a machine.

TOO OLD FOR THIS SHIT

On Bull Durham, *movies made by boomers, Clint Hurdle, finding one's path, and being, well, too old for this shit*

I'll do you the favour of not performing a complete accounting of all the rituals I attach to baseball. But as I write this in the brief, almost tremulous pocket between the start of spring training camps and the first tune-up games, I might as well tell you about one tradition: annually, at this point of almost unbearable anticipation for the season to come, I clear an evening, open a beer, and settle in to watch *Bull Durham*.

The glut of baseball movies made in the 1980s was, I have unscientifically concluded, a response to a demographic aberration. The baby boomers are the results of that glitch, and by the '80s they were approaching middle age. Baby boomers were established, property-owning, and in control. They weren't flower children anymore; they were bankers, real estate agents, producers, editors, studio executives. And as with anyone suddenly facing the downslope of their time on this planet, they had become aware of their own mortality. What followed was an attempt to find the sweet nexus of the innocence of their childhood, the idealism of their youth, and the hard realities of adulthood.

Baseball was a potent totem of innocence—a child's game, attached to early memories of Maris, Mantle, and Mays, and jamming cards into your bicycle spokes, and playing pickup games in dungarees and P.F. Flyers. Old baseball, that is, before artificial turf and polyester uniforms and designated hitters. Once boomers moved into the wheelhouse of the overburdened Icon-class cruise ship of culture, they were going to steer it toward their preferred destinations. First port of call? Nostalgia: There were going to be movies about ballplayers.

In 1984, Barry Levinson directed an adaptation of Bernard Malamud's novel *The Natural*, which mapped Arthurian legend onto the diamond. The film basks in schmaltz and fabulism (consider Roy Hobbs, portrayed by Robert Redford, smashing out the lights with a heroic slo-mo homer as Randy Newman's fanfare crescendos brassily). While the movie is affecting and well-acted, it smacks to me of the ultimately conservative notion that history rewards great men with triumph, thanks largely to an ending that deviates significantly from Malamud's text. The film was lauded, though, and paved the way for a wave of baseball movies that followed.

Eight Men Out (1988) is an excellent film by director John Sayles, based on Eliot Asinof's 1963 book of the same name about the 1919 White Sox. In Sayles's hands, the story is essentially about the loss of innocence—for the players, the game, and America as a nation. Made before much of the recent scholarship on the scandal, it repeats many of Asinof's assumptions in terms of the gullibility of the players and Charles Comiskey's apparent miserliness. None of this detracts from the movie's quality. It was a passion project for Sayles that captures the essence of the tale, presenting the story as convoluted and remarkably dour—as befits a story of such tragic corruption. It did not, however, capture the public imagination, flopping at the box office and receiving no award nominations. Its failure did nothing to dampen the studios' drive to make more diamond-set movies.

Field of Dreams, which uses those same Black Sox as a plot device, arrived in spring 1989. It was a runaway success, enjoying an eight-month theatrical run and earning three Oscar nominations. It's arguably the quintessential boomer baseball flick: Kevin Costner's Ray Kinsella, a former hippie who relocated to America's heartland and took up agriculture, literally uses baseball to bring back the ghost of his dead father, thereby reverting himself to a kind of arrested childhood and repairing their broken father-son relationship. James Earl Jones plays a role specifically adapted to differ from the source novel's (W. P. Kinsella's *Shoeless Joe*, for the record) depiction of the famously litigious J. D. Salinger. Timothy Busfield is in it. It is, plainly, boomer wish fulfillment writ large.

Also released in 1989, *Major League* is basically *Animal House* on the ball diamond, an R-rated comedy that scored at the box office and spawned sequels.

Into the midst of this surge of baseball movies dropped *Bull Durham*, released in 1988 and, like several of the above-named pictures, unquestionably a product of its age. It leans heavily on R & B, rock 'n' roll, and plaintive saxophone solos. There are neon bar signs. American-made cars signal virtue (Kevin Costner drives a vintage Mustang) while European cars stand as the ultimate mark of fey yuppiedom (Tim Robbins drives a Porsche) or affected sophistication (Susan Sarandon's Edith Piaf–listening, poetry-quoting Annie Savoy drives an old blue Volvo). As Crash Davis, Costner plays the no-nonsense everyman dispensing common-sense wisdom in the face of radical change. The world has gone mad, rocket-armed morons are getting millions, and only the old-school, rugged American individualist holds the key to sanity.

But *Bull Durham* never sinks under the weight of the film-making tropes of its very particular moment, and it doesn't succumb to sentiment. Unique among 1980s baseball movies, it locates the sweet spot, the perfect balance of cynicism and romanticism, and as a result it reads as authentic. Much of this is the result of writer-director Ron Shelton having spent five years in the minors—the California, Appalachian, Texas, and International leagues, plus a stint in the Florida Instructional League to boot. Shelton knew the bus leagues, the faint-hope outposts of the baseball landscape. He was a light-hitting 2B / SS with a .251 average and ten homers to his name. More importantly, he had the time to soak it all in—the players, the coaches, the fans, the parks, and the towns. This was his world and he poured it into *Bull Durham*.

Costner's Crash Davis is the weary veteran catcher sent down from AAA to the lowly Carolina League in order to babysit the hot young thing, pitcher Ebby Calvin "Nuke" LaLoosh (Tim Robbins). "I'm the player to be named later," says Davis when he appears in the dingy manager's office, duffel bag in hand, addressing bench coach Larry Hockett (who, as played by Robert Wuhl, is the funniest character in the movie), and manager Joe Riggins (the always excellent Trey Wilson).

Hockett's a clown who knows the game, an ex-pitcher who once served up a homer to Crash in the Texas League. He busies himself for much of this scene deflating an Oscar Mayer hot dog seat cushion. It's brilliant. Hockett's a guy, you sense, who might one day manage a team, but he's too loyal to those around him to show anything resembling ambition.

Skip Riggins carries himself with the gruff world-weariness of a man who has seen it all before, his feet up on the desk in his windowless office, a lit Marlboro in his hand and a cold High

Life within reach. But for all Riggins's wisdom, he finds himself at the end of his rope with a losing squad, and later says as much to Crash.

Crash's advice: "They're kids. Scare 'em." Riggins does just that, grabbing an armful of bats, tossing them in the showers, and ripping into the Bulls with exasperation and disdain. Our takeaway is that while Crash Davis is a sturdy veteran catcher with a small taste of the bigs, and a power hitter with the dubious distinction of sitting second on the all-time minor-league home run list, his real skill, and perhaps his true calling, is coaching.

Not that he's prepared for that. When brought up to speed on the particulars of his assignment—that is, mentoring LaLoosh—Davis balks. "I'm too old for this shit," he says.

★★★

On Saturday afternoon, August 16, 1986, the Cardinals were in New York to play the Mets, stuffing six games into four days, including a twin bill on Thursday and another on Sunday. The Cards were the reigning National League champs but had lost in seven to the Royals in '85's all-Missouri World Series. They were sitting around the .500 mark, sweating their way toward a third-place finish. The Mets were in first, thirty-five games over even, charging toward their eventual October date with the Red Sox, a series they'd take in seven games after Mookie Wilson's squibbler rolled through Billy Buckner's wickets.

But I'm getting ahead of myself. With the August 16 game scoreless, St. Louis first baseman Clint Hurdle led off the seventh inning, digging in against Dwight Gooden. Hurdle, a left-handed batter, fouled off Gooden's first pitch. At 0–1, Gooden reached back for some extra sauce and let fly a fastball that sailed up and in to Hurdle, who first tried to turtle his head into his shoulders, then belatedly began to turn away from the ball, which was already right on him. It pinged off his helmet, making a sound that can be replicated: go outside, find a rock that's somewhere between pebble- and fist-sized, and drop it from a second-storey window onto the lid of a metal trash can. That's a pretty close approximation of the sound Dwight Gooden's heater made ricocheting off Clint Hurdle's batting helmet.

"We'll hold our breath with you," said Bob Costas on the NBC *Game of the Week* broadcast while Hurdle lay prostrate. Mets catcher Ed Hearn—regular backstop Gary Carter was playing first that afternoon, giving his knees a break—crouched over Hurdle, leaning in, trying to communicate. Gene Gieselmann, the Cardinals' head trainer, shot out of the dugout and was quickly on his knees next to the fallen batter, who lay motionless, hands drawn to his face. Gieselmann dug smelling salts from his pocket and manoeuvred them under Hurdle's nose. Soon the tall utility man was awake, if not alert. He shook his head, turned away from the salts. A jet roared throatily overhead. In another moment, Hurdle was sitting up, looking around with a decidedly unfixed stare. Blood trickled from the cut that his helmet had opened above his right eye.

Hurdle had spent eight and a half big-league seasons playing wherever they put him: corner infield and outfield spots, pinch hitting, DH, catching. He came up with the Royals and played parts of five seasons for them, spent a year with the Reds, then portions of two season with the Mets, bisected by a full year at AAA Tidewater. The Cardinals siphoned him off New York in the Rule 5 draft after the 1985 season. He'd caught Gooden before but still hadn't expected that fastball to go where it went.

The blood was almost theatrical, running along Hurdle's brow and down his chiselled face. As he collected himself, sitting on the dirt of the left-handed batter's box at Shea Stadium, his thousand-yard stare beginning to resolve itself in the middle distance, he shook his head several times, possibly in response to a question proffered by Gieselmann or Cardinals manager Whitey Herzog, or maybe just as a reaction to his current predicament. A tick before he nodded his assent to being helped to his feet, there was a half beat in which you might plausibly surmise that Clint Hurdle, journeyman, either inside his recently rung bell or aloud under his breath, though only twenty-nine years old but with many, many baseball miles on his chassis, was expressing, in concurrence with fellow catcher Crash Davis, that he might, just possibly, be getting too old for this shit.

Hurdle took a few days off and was back in action on Wednesday, August 20, playing first and picking up a base hit against the Reds. He played three additional games in August and ten more before the season wrapped up, manning first, third, and serving as an occasional extra bat off the bench. As his crowded *Sporting News* index card has it, he was "Granted Free Agency 11/12." Three months later, the Mets picked him up again and once more assigned him to Tidewater. Hurdle would appear in just three major-league games in 1987, his last a 5–2 loss at Philadelphia on June 26. He entered the game to pinch hit in the pitcher's spot in the fifth inning. Kevin Gross struck him out looking. He was reassigned to Triple A ("rel. to Tidewater 7/1/87-") and hung 'em up at the close of the Tides' season. He bowed out with 32 big-league homers, 193 RBIs, a .259 average, an OPS+ of 106, and one stolen base.

Hurdle was a good ballplayer for whom things just didn't break the right way, so he never found the stardom that seemed like a sure thing when Kansas City took him in the first round of the 1975 draft. The pinched type on his index card charts his rise through the minors, progressing from rookie ball to A level, then jumping up to AAA in 1977. Later that season, as a September call-up, he homered in his first big-league game and finished the year with another homer and a .308 average in nine games. By spring training in 1978, he was considered enough of a phenom to appear on the cover of *Sports Illustrated*.

That was about as good as it got. In thirteen seasons he played 515 big-league games and 825 in the minors. His battle for spots mirrored his battle with alcoholism. Somewhere along the way, it must have occurred to Clint Hurdle that his playing days were numbered, but that he knew a lot about baseball and seemed to have a knack for passing that knowledge on to others. Coaching was his best shot to remain in the game. The Mets seemed to agree, making him the manager of their Florida State League team in Port St. Lucie ahead of the 1988 season. I'm willing to bet that if you know Clint Hurdle at all, you know him as a manager.

Just like he had as a player, Hurdle climbed the minor-league org chart, first with the Mets and then with the Rockies. By 1997, he was a big-league hitting coach. Early in the 2002 season, with the team already ten games below .500, the Rockies fired manager Buddy Bell and promoted Clint Hurdle. Hurdle steered Colorado for eight seasons, leading them to the 2007 World Series after a phenomenal run of twenty wins in twenty-one games, including the astonishingly exciting thirteen-inning tie-breaker game against San Diego that vaulted them into the playoffs after starting the month of September in fourth place in the NL West, six games behind the Padres. The Rockies were swept by the Red Sox in the Series, but they'd had a season for the ages.

The team disappointed in 2008 and started slowly in 2009, leading to Hurdle's dismissal. Texas hired him as a hitting coach for the 2010 season and rode a strong offensive campaign into the World Series, losing in five to the Giants. Hurdle was offered the keys to the Pirates after that and he stayed for nine seasons, during which he ended Pittsburgh's streak of twenty consecutive losing seasons, taking them to three straight Wild Card games. The Bucs backslid in the years that followed and Hurdle was dismissed in 2019, at which point he said he'd be stepping away from the game for a bit of rest.

Everywhere he went, at each level, people called him a teacher. Players, coaches, managers. It just seemed to be who he was. It only took him a few decades to figure it out.

★★★

There's not a lot I don't love about *Bull Durham*. It is, first of all, a film for grown-ups, with no merchandising and no fast-food meal tie-ins—an artifact from a time when Hollywood still made medium-budget original movies. It has a great script that, owing to Shelton's experiences, gets the minor-league vibe exactly right. It feels the way the minors used to feel: slapdash, chintzy, genuine.

The on-field action mostly passes the eye test, which isn't nothing. Robbins as LaLoosh has a pitching motion that's a little goofy but not implausible, while Costner moves like a ballplayer. They're surrounded by actual minor leaguers in the smaller roles, so nobody had to be taught how to hold a bat.

I can forgive the obvious errors too. The team announced as the Peninsula White Sox are clearly the Hagerstown Suns, and the Greensboro Hornets certainly existed but they were in the

Sally, not the Carolina League. In a way, spotting those things is some of the fun of repeated viewings.

But as Shelton writes in *The Church of Baseball*, his book about the making of the film, "What happens on the field is the least interesting part of the game." It's a koan that sports movies would do well to remember. If you want to watch a game, you'd just watch a game. Sports movies are inherently about the drama and comedy that plays out among the people involved. The games are more setting than focus. The best sports-related movies understand this.

For all the zingers (and there are a lot of zingers), the screwy meetings on the mound, and the comic sexual escapades, *Bull Durham* is a movie about growth. Nuke accepts tutelage, harnesses his freakish natural gifts, and gets promoted. Annie relents to her feelings, abandons her fervent personal rules, and allows herself to become vulnerable to love without an expiry date. Crash, meanwhile, accepts who he is and realizes that, as Shelton writes, he "loves something more than it loves him back." Crash sees to one last bit of baseball business before hanging up his chest protector, opens himself up to love, and admits that all along he's been on the wrong side of the player-coach divide—something Annie understood before he did. There's an opening for a manager in Visalia, Crash says, and maybe he'll put his name in.

This is another point at which the movie hews close to reality, because baseball is riddled with guys like Crash Davis—like Clint Hurdle—who teach from experience, but whose experience is not exactly festooned with garland. Their knees are shot, and their skin is leathery, and if they haven't had cataract surgery yet they soon will. They usually played in several levels of baseball—some, in fact, had a brief taste of life in The Show. But at each level, they were distinguished not necessarily by their skill but by their deep understanding of the sport. Sharing that knowledge ends up being their calling.

Bull Durham is about baseball, yes, but it isn't concerned with winning the big game or eulogizing a lost hero. It's about the process of discovering the difference between a vocation and an avocation, between a career and a calling. The movie is many things: romantic comedy, R-rated laff-fest, raunchy baseball flick. But ultimately, it's the story of a person's realization that who we've been isn't necessarily who we are, and that something we're pretty good at doesn't have to be our fate. Sometimes it turns out to be a means to an end.

LIVING SKIES

On loss, Mike Veeck, the St. Paul Saints, and corporate homogenization

From the fourth floor of a Best Western in Saskatoon, the April sky appeared fresh and newly unwrapped. The low skyline of the Paris of the Prairies knelt below a cool cerulean dome. Puffy white clouds scudded briskly, the whole scene one of constant change. *Living skies*, as the licence plates have it.

Christie and I were at the end of a very long drive undertaken somewhat hastily but necessarily, as her dear cousin Kevin had died suddenly of cancer. Kevin wasn't too much older than I am, which I think is what people mean when they say he died too young. But he *was* too young, and it was especially surprising for a guy who took good care of himself.

During our final email exchange, shortly before he died, he asked me what the hell had happened with the Jays during Game Two of their 2023 AL Wild Card series against the Twins. And, while we were talking ball, he also wondered how the Padres hadn't run away with the NL West in 2023, with all their talent—and could it be that saying "we're so incredibly good, we'll just reel off twenty wins in a row, starting tomorrow" isn't the same as *actually* being good?

I started by telling him that the real question was why the Jays had fallen to the third Wild Card spot to begin with—where were their big hitters? Otherwise, I shrugged and invoked the shorthand of sportswriting's laziest tropes: chemistry and luck. You can have everything lined up perfectly and still encounter the galloping spectre of chance. Plus, the Dodgers.

A father of three, Kevin's youngest is the same age as our oldest. Kevin had been raised on the East Coast and spent summers in PEI, the family cradle. He'd gone west for university, met a girl, settled in Saskatoon, found work in physiotherapy clinics. Loved travel, and jazz, and baseball, and his kids above all else. Did everything with enthusiasm. His illness progressed too fast to process. If someone who lived such a healthy life can succumb so quickly, what hope do the rest of us have? It's terrifying just to think about it.

The family was gathering in Saskatoon to mourn; the plan was for a funeral followed by an Irish wake. Curleys from Edmonton and the East Coast, Boyds from Manitoba, Brandts from Saskatchewan, all converged for this grief-letting and remembrance, hoping as people do that to spread around the sense of loss will somehow dilute it.

When Christie and I heard of Kevin's death, we sat with the news for a couple of days before concluding there was no way we couldn't be there. Financially speaking, we couldn't afford to fly both of us out, so we decided to drive. We entrusted the kids to their grandparents and hopped in the car. The drive took us thirty uneventful hours. We slept in shifts, a cooler full of food—sandwiches, granola bars, turkey sticks—tucked in the back seat so we could graze while driving, stopping only for gas. We left about midday from Peterborough and arrived in Saskatchewan late the next afternoon, the day before the service. The next morning, we pulled sombre vestments from a garment bag and walked across the street to the funeral home, where we were tearily greeted by some of our dearest relations.

Funerals inescapably inspire an inventory-taking; they remind you to hug your loved ones and so forth. When the person being honoured is within a decade of your own age, the event also feels like a shot across your bow. Kevin's memorial service was one of the most beautiful ceremonies I've ever attended. His parents, Jim (who'd gone to Royal Military College in Kingston and then served in the Navy with my dad) and Angela, did Bible readings and I was humbled by their strength. His brother, Colin, found humour and warmth in the midst of the whole unthinkable scenario. Kevin's beautiful children looked devastated—shocked, really—but were clearly aware that they were nested inside a family that would do all it could to support them.

Later, at the house some family members had rented on one of the apps, we gathered again, sharing hugs, stories, bottles, and even a few laughs. The next day, Christie and I lingered over the continental breakfast, said a few goodbyes, and climbed back in the car. We gave ourselves the small gift of a bit more time to make our way home. Time to wander a little, like we used to on the big road trips we took twenty, twenty-five years ago. On our way back, we'd take the scenic route.

★★★

On the Prairies, the flatness is broken in places where water has carved beautiful lines into the soft earth; because everything is relative, locally, they're called valleys. Out east, we'd call these features ravines or gullies or ditches. We traversed several of them as we drove south and east on arrow-straight roads. That particular part of the world seems purpose-built to facilitate the lifelong study of clouds, their varieties and characteristics, their behaviours: either daintily aloft, or darkening to brush the landscape with lacy hems, or to bear down and drag purple knuckles across the earth.

We passed beneath airborne flocks of geese in transit, cartoonishly small buffleheads struggling against a strong wind. Quail and pheasants dashed across desolate two-lane roads while Christie and I scanned the airwaves for sparse radio signals. I opened the MLB app and called up the audio of a ballgame, Dodgers at Twins. Freddie Freeman doubled to right, and Alex Kirilloff fielded it and fired to the cut-off man, who nailed Shohei Ohtani trying to score from first.

Grain cars bearing the insignia of the Wheat Board sat idle at remote and lonely railroad sidings. As we nosed south, they were gradually replaced by tanker cars and pumpjacks. At 120 kilometers per hour we flew past two moose standing in the saddest swale of trees you can imagine, the animals looking displaced and forlorn, the rain bearing down on us from the south.

We were briefly in Manitoba and then crossed the border into Antler, North Dakota. The Twins beat LA 3–2, and we switched over to terrestrial radio. An NPR anchor detailed another spike in consumer inflation as we wove through empty towns and fields pocked with winter stubble, no-cell-service country where other vehicles were few and far between. Bands of showers passed, then a rainbow planted itself across the horizon. "Stick Season" came on a station out of Minot and we shouted along.

If we'd had more time we might have done a tour of WGA ballparks of the Upper Midwest. Maybe one day I'll survey those tiny covered grandstands and fields that host high school, American Legion teams, or entries in summer collegiate leagues. You can lament the fact that many of them have had their grass and dirt replaced with million-dollar plastic carpet, but that's like saying new bands sound too much like watered-down Replacements cover acts. In the end, we ought to be happy that kids still form guitar bands with their friends.

Christie and I were headed toward the Twin Cities, though we wouldn't make it there in one day, so as I drove Christie scanned the internet to find us a hotel for the night, navigating comparison sites, third-party booking fees, and loyalty programs. When conducting a search like this, it hits you that so few companies actually own all these Red Roof Inns and La Quintas and Travelodges and Super 8s. The mom-and-pop spots of my memory are hard to find, if they still exist at all. In the end, we booked into a Days Inn by the interstate in Fargo.

Dinner was at a truck-stop diner on the outskirts of Grand Forks. The sunset over the parking lot was spectacular, dusky pinks and powdered purples, the clouds stretching beyond my peripheral vision in all directions. I had the meatloaf sandwich and a Dr. Pepper. We passed on dessert, and in darkness continued to Fargo and the room we'd rented, which featured a concrete slab of a bed, a broken toilet, and a heating/air-conditioning unit that sounded like a Sopwith Camel on start-up. But hey, it was only $80 for the night.

The next morning, in the breakfast nook off the lobby, we watched half an episode of *The Andy Griffith Show* while eating watery yogurt and prepackaged Danishes, then undertook the three-and-half-hour drive to the Twin Cities.

Our first stop was the Minneapolis Institute of Art. Highlights there included Winslow Homer, Gordon Parks's photos, a spectacular collection of Chinese landscape paintings on silk, and free admission. Then we crossed the Mississippi River to St. Paul, where the International League's Saints were gearing up to play the Iowa Cubs.

★★★

The St. Paul Saints have spent most of the last three decades in the independent minor leagues. In 1993, they were charter members of the Northern League, a circuit dreamed up by the tireless indie ball charlatan Miles Wolff, who brought the idea to Mike Veeck, son of Bill.

The junior Veeck had been trying to find his way back into baseball since his role in the White Sox's disastrous Disco Demolition Night promotion in 1979. The results of that night—injuries, arrests, destruction of property, the forfeiture of a game, and eventually his father's ouster from the ranks of big-league baseball ownership—had weighed heavily on the Sox's former director of promotions. The 1980s had been rough for Mike; he'd battled demons and the bottle, hung drywall, promoted jai alai, and waited for the phone to ring.

In 1989, New York lawyer Marvin Goldklang, investor Van Schley, actor Bill Murray, and singer Jimmy Buffett teamed up to buy the Miami Miracle of the Florida State League, a Class A team that was no one's first choice for a night out. Somebody suggested Mike Veeck's name to run them, and Goldklang took a flyer. A few years later, Wolff proposed putting a team in St. Paul and the same group bought in. Goldklang, impressed with Mike's energy from his time with the Miracle, offered him the top job with the Saints.

For Mike, the St. Paul job was an offer of nothing less than redemption. He jumped in with both feet, taking the reins and running the Saints with the fury of a man trying to make amends to family ghosts.

The squad took the field in 1993. The Saints name was adopted from several prior teams that have called St. Paul home. These included the 1890s Western League club that Charles Comiskey would move to Chicago and rename the White Sox and the minor-league organization that played in the American Association for sixty seasons until the Twins began playing in nearby Bloomington in 1961. From the outset, the Northern League, and the Saints in particular, operated as outsiders to affiliated ball, if not as outright outlaws. They were inheritors of an outlandish energy likely to result from a man named Veeck being allowed to steer a ballclub in an upstart league, far from the disapproving glares of the established order.

Most of the original Northern League teams were in the baseball hinterlands: Rochester, Minnesota; Sioux Falls; Sioux City; Thunder Bay; Duluth. And though St. Paul was just a handful of miles removed from the Hubert H. Humphrey Metrodome, home of the Twins, it offered something so radically different from its big-league neighbour that competition for local fans' dollars was unlikely. While the Twins sold expensive tickets to major-league games played on artificial turf beneath an inflatable dome, the Saints offered a cheap afternoon or night out, with last-chance players sliding, diving, and stumbling across real dirt and grass at tiny Midway Stadium, which Veeck christened "The Ugliest Ballpark in America."

Things couldn't have worked out better: Mike got his hands dirty painting fences, ripping tickets, dreaming up promotions, and generally living up to his last name while MLB teams were careening toward a work stoppage. When all the major-league stadiums, from the Bronx to Minneapolis to Chavez Ravine, were padlocked on August 12, 1994, kicking off the longest work stoppage in MLB history, baseball fans turned to the minors, both affiliated and otherwise.

Public perception identified pure greed as the root cause of the major-league labour dispute, and minor-league baseball seemed shielded from that blight; after all, it was barebones and skinflint, refreshingly modest and authentic by comparison. Fans' displeasure with MLB owners and players spilled over into the following seasons, and really only abated in 1998, when the Great National League Home Run Record Chase, starring Sammy Sosa and Mark McGwire, grabbed headlines. In the meantime, the minors flourished.

No team seemed more authentically modest or more further removed from the greed and excess of the majors than the St. Paul Saints. And though he spent most of his career toiling in the desert of independent baseball, Mike Veeck's last name wouldn't allow him to escape notice indefinitely. Which is what led Morley Safer and a *60 Minutes* crew to come calling in the summer of 1996.

The resulting segment, "St. Paul Saints vs. Major League Baseball," paints Veeck the younger in a flattering light, a maverick in his father's mould, a Barnumesque huckster in the great American tradition, and a charming rogue with a simple philosophy: fun is good. Mike positioned himself as the inheritor of a tradition of unearthing, creating, and sharing it: "A ballpark," he said, is "a celebration of humanity."

Part of the appeal, in Mike's eyes, and in Safer's, was that the Northern League was the end of the road as far as professional baseball was concerned. According to Safer, "Most of the Saints have two strikes against them before they even suit up."

Added Veeck, "When you show up at my door, you are at the

end of your career. I think that every one of these guys understand that this league is founded with the idea that there's one last hurrah in all of us." The Saints, and the independent leagues that would spring up over the next couple of decades, appealed to many fans precisely because of that energy: modesty, and the bright flare of the end of dreams.

A second chance is what Mike got, and that's what he was happy to dole out to a diverse collection of cast-offs, has-beens, and might-yet-bes. Among them was erstwhile Yankee Darryl Strawberry, who'd been suspended for a drug violation and was looking to work his way back into the game's highest level. Strawberry would play in twenty-nine games and hit eighteen home runs for the Saints before signing once again with New York on July 4. He remained in pinstripes while the Bombers won the Series, and for three more years after that.

Veeck and the others in Goldklang's group diversified, taking on minor-league teams in other leagues, eventually controlling five: the Saints, the Fort Myers Miracle (relocated from Miami), the Charleston RiverDogs, the Hudson Valley Renegades, and the Sioux Falls Canaries. But the Saints remained the jewel, winning three Northern League titles in five years.

And then suddenly Veeck got another shot at the majors. In 1998, the newly hatched Tampa Bay Devil Rays offered Veeck the post of senior vice president of marketing and sales. Who wouldn't take that? But he didn't love it; he kind of hated it. Around this time Rebecca, Veeck's seven-year-old daughter, was diagnosed with retinitis pigmentosa, a condition that would deteriorate her eyesight until it was completely gone.

So just months into the Devil Rays gig, he quit to take Rebecca on a year-long road trip to see everything she wanted to see while she still could.

Among their stops was Cooperstown, where Mike showed her a photo of Bill Veeck and Larry Doby, the man who integrated the American League. Said Rebecca, "Which one is Grandpa?"

At the end of their odyssey, Mike threw himself back into the minors where, like his dad, he reasoned that no promotion was too wacky. A game with no fans. A home-run derby on the deck of an aircraft carrier. The earliest start time in baseball history. A game without umpires. Pillow fights. Food fights.

Again, Veeck did it all. He tore tickets, spoke at every event that'd have him, helped the groundskeepers, answered phones. And Rebecca was right there, tearing tickets and answering phones too.

Years later, when more than her eyesight began to trouble her, she received a new diagnosis: Batten disease, a disorder with which vision problems are followed by behavioural changes, seizures, and worse. She continued to live in ballparks by her dad's side until, at the too-young age of twenty-seven, her fight ended.

★★★

A sharp, bright afternoon was losing its clarity as we crossed the Mississippi. The decorative flourishes on roadside sound barriers—chevron-shaped reliefs along perfectly linear stalks, suggesting wheat and progress both—drew our attention to the dark clouds rimming the eastern horizon. We found parking in downtown St. Paul and entered CHS Field, which had replaced Midway in 2015, and we double-checked the forecast. The chances of rain had ticked up, a proposition lent credibility by the eggplant clouds massing over centre and left. With an hour to go before first pitch, we wandered into the Saints' on-site museum just as the first drops began to fall.

Why doesn't every ballpark have a museum? The City of Baseball Museum makes a compelling case for their existence. Granted, the history of the game in the Twin Cities is especially rich. But I expect the same can be said for most every place that ball is played, if you dig deep enough.

The light rain abated and sun bathed the park, but the dark clouds lurked. I bought a hat, we got food, picked up lineups and a scorecard. We found our seats right behind the plate, nine rows up, and settled in.

It started to rain again, so we moved back a half-dozen rows until we were under the cover of CHS's hovering upper level, which kept us more or less dry. Most of the others in attendance did the same, and there was enough to watch on the field that we almost forgot about the cold.

The I-Cubs had arrived with some good players—Patrick Wisdom was playing first, rehabbing a sprained right wrist, while Pete Crow-Armstrong, the parent club's top prospect, manned centre. Iowa scored first when PCA led off with a single, took second on a wild pitch, stole third, then scored on a base hit, in a sequence of events I like to call a "Rickey Henderson." Time passed—damp, cool, and unscoring—until the sixth, when Saints shortstop Diego Castillo knocked one over the centre-field wall for a three-run homer. The Cubs answered that with a solo shot in the top of the seventh, making it 3–2 Saints.

In the bottom of the seventh, St. Paul centre fielder and leadoff hitter DaShawn Keirsey Jr. stepped in against Iowa lefty reliever Brad Wieck. Keirsey took a ball, fouled off two pitches, then took two more balls to run the count full. Wieck reared back and delivered a high four-seam fastball that was close enough that Kiersey had to swing. He fouled it back, over the screen. It sailed over the upper level of CHS Field and came down behind the last row of seats, in a plaza filled with wet, unoccupied tables and chairs. Christie had left our seats for a moment and I was alone, but I clearly saw the ball bounce and come to rest back there, with no one nearby, or at least no one particularly interested in crawling around in the puddles to find it. I walked over and made a half-hearted effort to find it but came up empty.

Wieck's next pitch was another four-seamer, a little lower but still near the top of the zone. Kiersey didn't miss it, depositing it far beyond the centre-field wall, way over PCA's head. Saints 4, I-Cubs 2.

★★★

I've been to a lot of baseball games, and nothing Christie and I saw between the lines that night in St. Paul was especially noteworthy. But Veeck's mark was all over the rest of experience.

Between innings there was an eyeball race, a golf chip shot competition, a dizzy bat race, and kids piloting out-of-control go-karts. Coach—a character and not, in fact, a coach—ran around in a sweatshirt, gym shorts, tube socks, and Chucks, sporting a moustache and aviators, a whistle around his neck. He led us in cheers, and gently chided us when the cheering did no good.

Seigo Masubuchi, an in-stadium "ushertainer," sang karaoke from the top of the Saints' dugout after the sixth inning, then led the crowd in the singing of "Take Me Out to the Ball Game" from the press box during the seventh-inning stretch while tossing out bags of peanuts to the clamouring masses (numbering in the low dozens by that point). I've read that Masubuchi once ran a marathon around the CHS Field concourse during a game; it took eighty-four laps.

Musical director and organist Andrew Crowley played from the press box. Nerd and Nerdette, Fanboy Fred, and the pink porcine mascot Mudonna and her safari tog–clad handler, Dawn Under, all roamed the aisles. And the *real* pig: each season on Opening Day the Saints introduce a piglet who will spend the season delivering fresh baseballs to the home-plate umpire. Each pig is given a unique name. On our visit, the porker was named Ozempig.

And all of this for an announced crowd of 3,028, which was in fact much smaller than that on a cold, wet Thursday night in April. The house that Mike Veeck built never had an off night.

These are all hallmarks of the Saints game-day experience—silly, schmaltzy, goofy, wonderful—and if some of them are familiar it's either because someone named Veeck invented them, or someone else did and a Veeck perfected it. As Bill Murray once told a local TV reporter, "Everything we started doing here in the 1990s, all the major-league teams do now in their ballparks."

★★★

In the Veecks' wake, the minor leagues became both hotbeds of baseball talent, and folksy, community-built sources of family entertainment. But all good things must come to an end.

In 2020, with the world in the throes of a pandemic, big-league teams played games in empty parks and minor-league teams saw their seasons cancelled. To this point, minor-league baseball had operated with a reasonable degree of freedom, with individual teams signing player development agreements with big-league clubs. But during that lost season, Major League Baseball, under Commissioner Rob Manfred, assumed universal control of the minor leagues, bringing in a new, standardized Player Development League (PDL) structure, in which affiliated minor-league clubs signed ten-year contracts. New facility standards were established and levels reorganized. Gone were short-season leagues like the New York–Penn. Some previously independent teams became affiliates, and forty-three minor teams were eliminated. The MiLB office in St. Petersburg, Florida, was shuttered, its operations moved into MLB's headquarters in New York. If all this sounds like a corporate takeover homogenizing what had been independent operations with local flavour, well, that's precisely what it is. Manfred also spoke of a plan he called "One Baseball," under which MLB owners would exercise control over all aspects of the game, from Little League on up.

The Saints were among the independent teams elevated to affiliated status; they became the Twins' top farm club, moved into the Triple A East (which later reverted to its historic moniker, the International League), and left their independent circuit days behind.

Shortly after the announcement, likely sensing a bubbling anxiety among the Saints' faithful, the team's media relations guy, Sean Aronson, and Derek Sharrer, executive VP and GM, held a livestream to address fans' concerns. They stressed that the people who worked for the Saints would stay with the Saints—other than players and coaching staff, who would be replaced by coaches and players within the Twins' organization. Aronson and Sharrer reassured the public that the game-day experience would stay the same. They insisted that prices would stay low. "Within the Saints' DNA is affordability," said Sharrer.

Live games returned to the minors in 2021, and Veeck and company held on to the Saints for two more seasons before agreeing to sell the team to a group called Diamond Baseball Holdings.

Briefly, because this stuff bores me as much as it does you: DBH, funded by the private equity firm Silver Lake, was spawned in 2021 and immediately bought up ten minor-league teams. Part and parcel of the MLB takeover of the minors, by the way, was the eradication of the rule that you couldn't own more than one team in a given league. Since everything was overseen by Manfred's men, they figured, there was no room for shenanigans like those pulled by the ownership syndicates of the nineteenth century, like stripping players from one team to load up the other. So DBH could buy, and buy, and buy. Thanks to a "strategic partnership" with MLB aimed at bringing in more sponsorships and branding opportunities that would increase revenue, big-league owners were happy with this arrangement. By the time Christie and I attended that Saints–I-Cubs game, DBH had collected thirty-two clubs, including both of the teams we were watching.

The modern consumer is inundated with opportunities to support once-independent entities that have been subsumed by larger players. It's the evolutionary cycle we have, if not the one we deserve, and it touches everything from craft breweries to modes of entertainment distribution and, now, minor-league baseball. Where something succeeds because of its relationship with the admittedly hazy notion of authenticity, a siphonophore of capital will float over to absorb it, then seek to make copies of whatever made the original entity successful.

Something is always lost in the process. In this case, the hyper-localism of minor-league baseball teams—the peculiar relationship each has to its community, the regional quirks, and the inefficient yet charming characteristics of the enterprise—will likely be bulldozed in order to standardize the operation. These sorts of arrangements always result in "opportunities for synergistic exchanges" or whatever, which in plain speak looks like the 2024 promotion where every single minor-league team, across all levels, played one game in a uniform that was nothing more than a wearable billboard for a brand of oat milk. For those in charge, this flattening of the experience is an acceptable trade-off for the money they stand to make.

I can't say with certainty that all happened in St. Paul since I'd never been to a game before the sale. It felt good to be there. It was fun, and never once did I get the impression that any of the zany antics I was enjoying had been cooked up in a Manhattan meeting room. And I do believe that the people on the ground, operating teams in places like St. Paul, Minnesota, or Everett, Washington, or Amarillo, Texas, continued to work in good faith and with the aim of maintaining a genuine relationship with the people in those communities. But it does not seem to me the sort of environment in which the next Veeck would thrive.

As for the affordability that is within the Saints' DNA? One might chalk it up to post-Covid inflation, but I've paid less for both tickets and food at some major-league games.

And I know this: late in the 2023 season, after DBH had taken control of the team, the Saints held a celebration of the group that had owned the team since its 1993 inception—Bill Murray, Goldklang, Veeck, and company. Darryl Strawberry was on hand to have his number retired and to say nice things about the team and the community. When a local reporter asked Mike Veeck if he had any regrets about selling, Mike teared up. "This is half my life," he said, "so I have regrets."

★★★

The reasons we attend memorial services aren't all that different from the reasons we attend baseball games: to connect with and affirm our place in a group. It comforts me to know that we still do these things, that we gather for love, and for fun, and for the safety of a crowd.

Christie and I had gone west to be with family, to share pain and love with our familiars, the people who knew us when, and will know us until. And we'd gone home by way of St. Paul because we wanted to share space with our old selves, the people we'd been all those years ago, burning miles, sleeping in the passenger seat, singing along with the radio as the late-afternoon sun sneaks through a break in a thunderhead while we race across the Great Plains or the Upper Midwest, hoping to hit the next town in time to catch a minor-league baseball game.

All of this commingled as we watched the Saints and the I-Cubs. The leisure of a place you've never really been, the lifelong work of grief. The happiness to be found in the ways you change alongside the people you love most, and the ways you stay the same.

The Cubs tacked on another run in the seventh on a sac fly, and held on to win 5–2. On our way out of CHS Field, I spotted the ball that DaShawn Keirsey Jr. had fouled into the damp, dim plaza, the bright orb sitting beneath a table, clear as day. I walked briskly over and picked it up, rolled it around in my hands, and showed it to Christie. I couldn't contain my giddiness; I was as happy as a ten-year-old boy.

The ball was surprisingly clean, with no major scuffs or faults, just a bit of dirt and a small blemish near the label, which was stamped in blue ink that read:

OFFICIAL
MAJOR LEAGUE BASEBALL
Robert D. Manfred Jr.
COMMISSIONER

I put the ball in the pocket of my raincoat, pulled the hood over my new Saints cap, and we made our way toward the car. Then we made our way out of the Twin Cities, merging onto the interstate and heading east. We drove through heavy darkness and a bit of rain. Wind rattled our licence plates and bent the antenna as we gassed up and bought cold canned espresso drinks and tubes of potato chips at an all-night gas station. We drove around Chicago, down along the bottom of Lake Michigan.

We'd driven westward in a blur, pulled by the need to be with family, and the same need drew us home. Through Gary, Kalamazoo, Lansing. Dawn cast a dim, diffuse light on a damp morning, and we drove on, crossed the border at Sarnia. Fifteen hours we drove, still ringing with loss but bolstered by love. The 401 to the 407 to the 115, hungry and dazed, but spurred by something blood-borne, something we both understood without needing to speak it. Like mad people we drove, running on fumes, singing our favourite songs, because we had it in our heads that we wanted to be home when the kids got back from school.

TELL ME ABOUT HEAVEN

On Sam Nahem, the twentieth century, and dreaming of a better world

John, my father-in-law, came over the other day because our automatic garage door opener was being funny. I'd press the button and it would go all the way down and then, once it hit the ground, it would go all the way back up again. John and I looked at the motor, and the track and chain, and then closely and specifically at the little doohickey—imagine a uvula made of flimsy plastic, just hanging there, wiggling a bit—that was screwed by a bracket onto the overhead track. The uvula thing, when nudged by the carriage moving along the track, was supposed to signal the motor to stop, pressing a brittle little wire into a contact. But the uvula was old and bent. And so, instead of pushing it, the carriage brushed it aside, the wire didn't move, and the door kept going until it hit the ground, forcing the motor to stop and begin to reverse.

My father-in-law is a doer, a tinkerer, a clever man with a keen scientific and practical mind. There really isn't anything he won't try to fix. It's an admirable trait. He ran the door up, and then down, and back up, and so on, looking at things closely before deciding we could use duct tape and an L-bracket to beef up the plastic uvula so that the carriage would push the wire and stop the door. We doubled the duct tape for durability and then stood back, pressed the button, and watched.

Sure enough, the door rolled all the way down, tripped the uvula, which pressed the wire home. The door stopped exactly where it was supposed to. Fixed. Among all of John's repairs that I've assisted with, this was perhaps the least elegant, but it worked, and that's the only true test of a repair's efficacy.

The site of this great triumph fits one of our two cars (a Hyundai Elantra) and is otherwise filled with many bicycles (we have two bikes for every one person in the household, for reasons I can't fully explain), two lawn mowers, twenty Frisbees, seven basketballs, oil of all varieties (auto, two-stroke, four-stroke, chainsaw bar, bike chain grease, etc.), flowerpots, hedge trimmers, pieces of salvaged furniture we'll one day refinish, maybe, and all other manner of stuff. The garage is in Peterborough, attached to the second house Christie and I have owned. We closed on the property in August 2008, on the eve of the Great Recession, using equity we'd accumulated with our first house in Oxford Mills, which we'd bought in the weeks after 9/11.

The house in Peterborough is essentially where we've raised our kids, a late-1970s split-entry three-bedroom close to a good elementary school. Fenced yard, a couple of maples out front, plenty of room to throw and hit a baseball, close to parks and playgrounds, basketball courts.

All of this together—the space filled with decades' worth of accumulated junk, the real estate transactions in relatively soft housing markets, and the power tools we've used to fix up, remodel, and maintain the house—seems redolent of the twentieth century. I've had a good run in the twenty-first, marrying, having children, scratching together a career, easing into middle age. But I'm unquestionably a product of the twentieth, my values forged in the death throes of that gonzo century with its hot stew of monumental violence, unprecedented affluence, and absolute poverty. Mass media, total war, rampant mechanization, proto-digitization, civilizational-level ideological struggle, and high mass production: it was, in ways both good and very bad, a hell of a century, and everything I know was touched by it.

★★★

Sam Nahem was also a product of the twentieth century, shaped by its early and midpoints, though he lived through 85 percent of it. Like me, Nahem dreamed of a better world. Unlike me, he expended a great deal of energy trying to bring it about.

Nahem was born in New York City in 1915, the son of Syrian Jews who'd left Aleppo three years earlier. He grew up speaking Arabic before learning English, though once he mastered American idioms he was off to the races. A voracious reader, young Sam excelled both in the classroom and on the field. He played football as well as baseball, where he began as a catcher. He had trouble fitting the mask over his glasses, so he switched to pitching.

He was recently bar mitzvahed when his father, Isaac Nahem, successful in the import-export business, sailed aboard the liner SS *Vestris*, a 511-foot-long steamer en route from New York to the River Plate. On November 12, 1928, the *Vestris*, overloaded with coal, went down off Norfolk, Virginia, taking over a hundred people with her, including Isaac.

Nahem's family sued the steamship company, and the settlement helped them remain solvent during the oncoming Great

Depression. Sam's efforts to share his wealth by distributing heating coal among his less well off relatives suggested a practical sensibility—using what was at hand to fix a problem he recognized—and formed his early understanding of socialism.

Nahem had a cousin active in the Communist Party, and once done high school Sam entered Brooklyn College, a nexus of new ideas, activism, and the lure of change. He was drawn to literature, music, and radical politics. He joined the Communist Party, wore round wire glasses, and employed an unconventional throwing approach: overhand to lefties and sidearm to righties.

Nahem's activism flowered in an age of crisis and advancement, as the previous several decades had seen strikes by coal miners, steelworkers, police officers, oil field roughnecks, mill workers, textile workers, auto workers. There were arrests, brawls, murders, riots, massacres. The US Supreme Court upheld the legality of "yellow-dog" contracts, which included stipulations that workers not join unions nor engage in any union-like activity. Two successive child labour laws were struck down, but eight-hour days became the norm. The Industrial Workers of the World formed in 1905, while the Communist Party of America started in 1919, the product of a rift within the Socialist Party of America on the heels of the Russian Revolution. This is the crucible of labour and politics that formed Nahem's outlook.

After his sophomore year, Nahem—as the card index lists him, "Nahem, Samuel Ralph... wearsXXglasses"—finagled a tryout with the Brooklyn Dodgers. Manager Casey Stengel liked what he saw, signed the kid, and sent him to traipse around the lower minors, including the NY–Penn, Evangeline, Three-I, and Eastern leagues. Sam also began to read for a law degree at St. John's University in New York, despite not having finished his degree at Brooklyn College, a fact that suggests both intellect and moxie.

In his unpublished autobiography, Nahem described the minors as "hot dusty bush leagues" characterized by "long night bus travel, small crowds, crummy food, small time love affairs." He dealt with the boredom and isolation by reading. "What does one do in Columbus, Ohio for the summer? The complete works of Honoré de Balzac. What about Jeanerette, Louisiana? Of course, the complete works of Theodore Dreiser." His minor-league teammates, many of whom had never met a genuine New Yorker, took to calling him Subway Sam.

In the 1930s, the Spanish Civil War raged. The National Socialist Party took power in Germany. Mussolini's fascism had a stranglehold on Italy; totalitarianism's zealots framed it as a bulwark against the libidinal chaos described by Freud, using Henry Ford's micro-division of labour to maintain a state designed to check the desire for total freedom embodied by Cadillacs and "degenerate" art. And then, on the last day of the 1938 season, Nahem got his shot with the Dodgers, pitching against the Phillies at Shibe Park. Brooklyn was bad that year; the Phillies were worse. Nahem beat them 7–3, surrendering six hits and going 2-for-5 with an RBI at the plate. He earned his law degree and passed the bar that December, the end result of all that studying between games, between seasons, in the minors and the majors.

The Dodgers, eying a turnaround the next season, opted not to keep the young hurler on the roster, shipping him to Montreal where the Royals were managed by grizzled vet Burleigh Grimes, who taught Nahem a slider before Sam was shuffled to Nashville by the parent club. He was called up in August but saw no action before reassignment back to

Tennessee. That's where Sam was, toiling away in the Southern Association, when Hitler crossed into Poland.

Nahem pitched poorly in spring training 1940 and the Dodgers intended to ship him back to AA Nashville. But Sam, feeling he'd proven himself, negotiated for a transfer to the Louisville Colonels. His confidence in these dealings stemmed from having what so few players could claim: a fallback plan. If the Dodgers tired of his antics, he could walk away from the game and start a law practice.

The Colonels were a Red Sox affiliate, but Brooklyn retained Nahem's rights—temporarily. A couple months into the season, they traded him to the Cardinals in a package that netted the Dodgers Ducky Medwick. St. Louis shunted Nahem to their minor-league team in Houston. Jostled around, he righted himself and pitched well enough to help the Buffs win the Texas League title.

At last, in 1941, Sam Nahem broke camp with a big-league club, travelling north as a St. Louis Cardinal. After a couple of solid outings as a reliever, Nahem made good in his first start, on April 23 at Sportsman's Park, beating the Pirates 3–1, going the distance and giving up just three hits and a lone walk while fanning three. The outing was "the greatest game I ever pitched," Nahem would later say. "Tell me about heaven."

Nahem started eight games and pitched as a reliever in eighteen that season for St. Louis, going 5–2 with a 2.98 ERA. Somehow it wasn't good enough and the Cards bumped him down to AA Columbus, though Sam threatened to not report; he may have been thinking once again about that law practice. But report he did, though he might have been better off sticking to his guns; down the stretch he went winless with an ERA north of 9.

That offseason, St. Louis sold Nahem to the Phillies. He

appeared in thirty-five games in 1942 for a last-place club that would finish a disastrous 62.5 games back. When the season wrapped up, Sam enlisted.

He was stationed at Fort Totten, New York, a corporal in the anti-aircraft section of the Eastern Defense Command. The following spring, Nahem played baseball for the Anti-Aircraft Redlegs, pitching to an ERA of 0.85 and playing every position but catcher. He was sent to France toward the end of 1944 and was still there when hostilities came to a halt in May 1945.

After the fighting ended, hundreds of thousands of American troops remained in Europe. Baseball was among their off-duty pastimes. Now-sergeant Nahem ran leagues for servicemen in Reims, France, and managed and pitched for the Overseas Invasion Service Expedition (OISE) All-Stars, a team that proved worthy enough to advance to the European Theater of Operations (ETO) World Series come September.

Servicemen's teams were seldom racially integrated, but at Nahem's insistence his OISE squad featured Negro League stars Leon Day, a pitcher who'd most recently been with the Newark Eagles, and outfielder Willard Brown of the Kansas City Monarchs (both are now Hall of Famers). In the best-of-five championship, they matched up against an all-white team stocked with major leaguers representing the 71st Division of Patton's Third Army. Beaten handily in the first game, the OISE All-Stars fought back in Game Two thanks to a Leon Day pitching gem. Game Three was Nahem's time to shine on the mound, outduelling Ewell Blackwell (who pitched for the Cincinnati Reds during peacetime) for a 2–1 victory.

The 71st got to Day in Game Four to tie the series, necessitating a deciding fifth game to be played at "Soldiers' Field" in Nuremberg, which was the new designation for the

Zeppelinfeld structure located in the northeast corner of the enormous Nazi Party rally grounds. Crowned with an enormous golden swastika, the Zeppelinfeld was the Albert Speer–designed assembly ground enclosed within a horseshoe grandstand and a vast straight colonnade. Hitler staged six rallies there, and the chilling images of saluting Nazis in rapt adoration of the ranting demagogue while surrounded by Speer's Cathedral of Light—a display of 152 anti-aircraft searchlights pointed skyward, suggesting a monumental architecture that dwarfed those assembled—are among the most infamous to have emerged from the Second World War. The use of the grounds for baseball games attended by over fifty thousand spectators was a powerful rebuke of the Nazi program and an affirmation of the American way of life. It must have been a particularly poignant experience for Nahem, the New York Ashkenazi Jewish ballplayer.

Nahem started Game Five, but he got into trouble in the fourth inning and replaced himself with Bob Keane, who stopped the bleeding and completed the game. The OISE eked out another 2–1 victory, winning the series. *The Sporting News* report on the game was accompanied by a photo of Nahem.

Stateside, a month after Leon Day and Willard Brown won the ETO World Series, Branch Rickey announced the Dodgers' signing of Jackie Robinson.

★★★

Sam Nahem was discharged in early 1946. He was thirty years old, and though the Phillies still held his rights (thank you, reserve clause), Nahem was without a baseball job. He had a few false starts—law clerk, his family's import-export business—but he soon embarked down two new paths: a new legal practice and semipro baseball.

He joined the Brooklyn Bushwicks, an independent club that filled its schedule with matches against barnstorming Negro League teams, minor-league sides, and other semipro squads. He also lent his skills on a part-time basis to the Sunset Stars of Newport, Rhode Island, all while practising law. Nahem managed to patch together a life on his own terms. He also set aside time in the winter to play for the Navegantes del Magallanes club of the Venezuelan Professional Baseball League. Nahem would later tell a reporter that the combined income of his stints with these three teams amounted to more than he'd ever made in the bigs.

He maintained his semipro status in 1947, but in 1948, while with the Bushwicks, the Phillies rang him up. On April 30, he once again found himself in the National League, entering in the eighth inning against the Dodgers, who held a 7–2 lead. He pitched two innings of mop-up duty. The results—that afternoon and thereafter—were underwhelming, though the fact that Philadelphia was in the midst of its sixteenth consecutive losing season surely lifts some of the responsibility off Sam's shoulders. He also clashed with Ben Chapman, the Phils' notoriously racist and pugnacious manager. Nahem pitched his last major-league inning on September 11, against Boston's NLers. A week later, the Phillies cut him loose.

He went back to his ad hoc arrangement in 1949, spending time with the Bushwicks and occasionally hopping on a train down to Newport to moonlight for the Sunset Stars. In June, he played a thirteen-inning game in Rhode Island, caught an early morning train, and arrived back in New York just hours before his wedding to Elsie Hanson, an art student he'd met at a Communist Party fundraiser.

Working as a law clerk, Nahem remained active in leftist politics, even as the spectre of McCarthyism loomed. He was a member of the American Labor Party, and protested the espionage conviction of Ethel and Julius Rosenberg. He hoped to provide legal counsel in the area of civil liberties but found work hard to come by. While he looked for an in, he improvised by doing door-to-door sales, working as a longshoreman. But jobs disappeared quickly because the FBI, who'd had him under surveillance, kept tipping employers to his involvement with the Communist Party.

Eventually, Sam went west. He moved to the Bay Area with Elsie and their two kids, and found work at a fertilizer plant, where he stayed for twenty-five years. He continued to organize, becoming active in the Oil, Chemical and Atomic Workers Union, and refusing any promotion that would force him to leave the union.

In 1964, the family moved to Berkeley, which was quickly becoming a hive of activism. Sam attended anti-war protests and civil rights demonstrations. In 1969, he participated in a nationwide strike among Standard Oil workers that turned violent when the Rockefeller-owned company sent in strikebreakers.

Elsie died of cancer in 1974; Sam retired from the plant in 1980, took a volunteer position at the UC Berkeley Art Museum. When he died at eighty-eight, in 2004, his family requested donations in his name be made to Doctors Without Borders—one more practical, community-minded act on Sam's behalf.

★★★

Shortly after we fixed the automatic door, I undertook a purging of the garage, combing through decades of junk to sort the still useable from the obsolete. I did donation runs, recycling runs, a load of hazardous waste, then filled a trailer with the rest (scrap lumber, deflated basketballs, concrete rubble, a leaky garden hose) and drove out to the local landfill.

Seagulls pinwheeled overhead, lazy formations of them riding pungent updrafts. Of all the dumps I've known, our local is the sleekest. The "architecture of waste," writes Don DeLillo in *Underworld*. How we engineer our piles of garbage, sift it, silo it. The small-town dump in Eastern Ontario, near our first house, was just a pile. You drove up it, stopped, chucked stuff onto the heap, and drove off. More recently, waste relay stations I've visited have instituted systems of apportionment: concrete stalls, this one for building materials, that one for yard waste, this one for metal. My local landfill, south of Peterborough, requires careful sorting into a dozen roll-off bins resting in the shadow of the vented and sod-enclosed, plateau-topped hill filled with decades of garbage. Beyond, a colony of bulldozers flattens, massages, caresses the current landfill site, treating with care and deference the spillover of our lives of staggering plenty.

It's a strange place to think of Sam Nahem. But he comes to mind because, just as I've come to think of waste management as a quintessential byproduct of the twentieth century, I consider Nahem an exemplar of his tumultuous age.

A child of immigrants, a ballplayer, barrister, activist, soldier, lover of art and literature, and trade unionist, his life took him from New York to a bunch of minor-league towns to the stadiums of the National League, from wartime France to the rally grounds of Nuremberg, and a long final act in California.

His century began with red tunics and bolt-action rifles, was bisected by the development and proliferation of doomsday weapons, and ended with mass surveillance and forever wars waged by unmanned aerial vehicles raining Hellfire missiles onto oil-rich desert landscapes. It gave us fauvism, cubism, abstract expressionism, and meat dresses. It birthed universal suffrage, the World Series, Hollywood, and the Civil Rights Act; it countered itself with pandemics, authoritarian governments, environmental ruin, and twenty-four-hour distraction. Such tenebristic contrasts are not unique to the twentieth century, though it did perhaps take things to an unseemly extreme.

Sam Nahem's life spanned that chaos, and through it all he maintained his ideals and set his own terms. He eschewed the prevailing Western heroic vision of the individual and instead viewed himself as part of the puzzle, communally responsible for the betterment of the lives of those around him and those who'd come after him. In a century of warring ideologies, calls and responses, theory and debate, Sam Nahem, a righty with a decent slider, lived a life of action and organizing. His lifetime big-league record was ten wins and eight losses, though if ever there was a career that statistics fail to adequately describe, it's Subway Sam's.

Baseball and activism are hard slogs, dealing failure far more commonly than they dole out triumph, but they're both, at heart, endeavours rooted in hope. Sam's idea was that, with hard work, he might prove to be of some use as a soldier in an army tasked with bringing the fallen, imperfect world a little closer to the paradise it might be.

A HOLE IN THE WIND

On Britt Burns's well-deserved ovation in the tenth inning of Game Four of the 1983 ALCS

Surrounded by his colleagues, Britt Burns prepared to go to work. It was a blustery and overcast afternoon, the flags darting erratically, napkins and hot-dog wrappers whipping across the field. At game time, just after noon, the temperature was fifty-seven degrees Fahrenheit. Those filing into Comiskey Park, the Baseball Palace of the World, shivered in the chill and snap of October baseball.

"Pretty good breeze, kinda blowing in from centre field," said Baltimore TV announcer Chuck Jones. Next to him in the booth, ex-Orioles third baseman Brooks Robinson provided colour commentary.

The date was October 8, 1983, and the occasion was Game Four of the American League Championship Series between the White Sox and the Baltimore Orioles. Since moving from St. Louis to Baltimore in 1954, the ex-Browns had won five pennants and two World Series. They'd just earned the AL East title by finishing six games ahead of the Tigers at the end of the 1983 regular season.

Meanwhile the White Sox hadn't sniffed a pennant since 1959, when they'd lost the World Series to the Dodgers. Their last title was in 1917. And Chicago had started slow in 1983—they sat at 20–25 on June 1, then went 18–10 that month. They kept their heads above water in July, and then something clicked. The Sox were 22–9 in August and 22–6 in September, eventually wrapping up the West with a twenty-game lead over the Royals. The turnaround was partly due to the outstanding offensive seasons turned in by veteran catcher Carlton Fisk, first baseman Tom Paciorek, left fielder Ron Kittle (later named Rookie of the Year), young right fielder Harold Baines, and big DH Greg "the Bull" Luzinski. As a team, they'd lead the AL in runs scored that year.

But the Sox's real strength was their rotation of LaMarr Hoyt, Richard Dotson, Floyd Bannister, Britt Burns, and Jerry Koosman. Other than the forty-year-old Koosman, it was a young group—Hoyt and Bannister were twenty-eight, and Dotson and Burns twenty-four. Hoyt followed up a good season in '82 with a very good one in '83, leading the league in wins at 24–10, staying healthy and generally not walking hitters. At the cessation of hostilities, Hoyt would be handed the AL Cy Young Award. In all, the five Chicago starters pitched to a 3.71 ERA, the third-best staff in the league by that metric. They started 155 games and accounted for 83 of the Sox's 99 wins.

The best-of-five League Championship Series (the current best-of-seven format started in 1985) kicked off at Baltimore's Memorial Stadium. In Game One, a brilliant Hoyt went the distance, surrendering only five hits and one run in a 2–1 win. In Game Two, Bannister faltered, giving up four runs (three earned) while the Orioles' Mike Boddicker pitched a lights-out game, striking out fourteen while giving up no runs and finishing the ninth himself. Final: 4–0.

Game Three at Comiskey was ugly: Dotson gave up six runs, including a first-inning three-run shot by Eddie Murray. A string of three relievers couldn't do much better. Final: 11–1, putting Baltimore up 2–1 in the series. They were looking to wrap things up with Game Four on that windy Saturday afternoon in the South Side of Chicago.

For Game Four, Baltimore manager Joe Altobelli tabbed lanky Storm Davis, a second-year righty from Jacksonville, Florida. White Sox helmsman Tony La Russa countered with Burns.

Robert Britt Burns was born in Houston but grew up in Birmingham. He grew up too fast, in fact, causing damage to his hips. Surgery to stabilize the joints kept him out of school for a year, but when eventually he returned to playing ball, he dominated his high school peers, surrendering a lone earned run in his final two seasons. That brought the scouts to Birmingham for a game Burns was set to pitch on a rainy day. He did little to impress them beyond allowing no hits and striking out eighteen.

Burns already had a scholarship offer from Auburn in his back pocket, but that performance allowed him to imagine being drafted sooner rather than later. It's funny, then, that it wasn't a scout's recommendation that got him on the Sox's radar, and which eventually saw them pick him in the third round of the 1978 draft. Instead, Burns owed thanks to *Chicago Tribune* book critic Bob Cromie. While passing through Birmingham, Cromie sent a local newspaper clipping back to Bill Veeck, who then sent a scout to check the kid out. The scout liked what he saw.

Burns got knocked around in two big league starts in '78. He appeared in six games for the Sox the next year, and by 1980 he was a full-time big leaguer. His stuff played in the majors; he went 15–13, pitched 238 innings, struck out 133, and notched a trim ERA of 2.84.

In July, he appeared alongside two co-workers, Ross Baumgarten and Steve Trout, on the cover of *Baseball Digest*, three baby-faced young men in the early stages of their professional careers. Wearing the Sox's goofy, second-Veeck-era butterfly-collared jerseys, they posed awkwardly, holding balls before them in half-hearted pantomime of their pitching motions. Above them blared the all-caps headline "LEFTY PITCHERS BRIGHTEN WHITE SOX FUTURE."

At the end of the season, La Russa went to bat for Burns, campaigning on his lefty's behalf. "If that kid's not Rookie of the Year, there's no such thing," he said. The baseball writers saw things a different way, handing the award to Cleveland's Joe Charboneau. Burns finished fifth. But he was recognized by the fraternity of ballplayers; he was named the Rookie Pitcher of the Year, an award voted on by his fellow players. He shaved his ERA down to 2.64 in 1981 and was named to the AL All-Star squad. In *Sports Illustrated*, Jim Kaplan wrote, "if Chicago has a future, Burns seems to be it."

If Burns's 1982 performance represented a bit of a backslide, he showed signs of righting himself in 1983. And he had a chance to keep his team's season alive on that Saturday afternoon.

Buffeted by strong winds, Burns stood on the Comiskey mound, ready to deliver to Orioles centre fielder John Shelby. The hurler was big-framed though not bulky, with a boyish mop of curly brown hair stuffed beneath his tritone cap, the navy SOX against the white front panel. Owing to his hip troubles, Burns still walked with a hitch, but none of that was apparent in his pitching motion, which began with an unhurried step back, his hands coming together slowly over his head, a big kick of his right leg, a quick lunge forward, and then the whipping of his big left arm.

"And the first pitch from Britt Burns is ball one," said Chuck Jones, "and here we go in Game Four." At 2–2, Shelby slapped a bounding ball to Vance Law at third, whose throw to first was a hair late. A leadoff single might have seemed an auspicious beginning to the 45,000 folks settling into their cramped seats, but the second hitter, right fielder Tito Landrum, bunted too hard and too straight, allowing Burns to field it, wheel, and nab Shelby at second. Burns then got Cal Ripken Jr. to ground one to short for a quick double play. No need for alarm.

In the bottom half of the inning, Storm Davis retired Rudy Law on a ground ball to second, then gave up a single to catcher Carlton Fisk. Known as the Commander, Fisk was smart, stern, and fearless, but not fast; Harold Baines was next up and his line drive to short made for an easy double play.

The tone of the game was set. Zeros propagated like dandelions on Comiskey's scoreboard. Burns gave up a single and walk in the second, then went strike out, fly out, ground out. In the bottom half, Davis worked around a walk to keep the scoreless tie.

At no point did Burns ever appear to feel any urgency. "Burns labors like a monk over a manuscript," observed *Sports Illustrated*'s Jim Kaplan. I sense that Burns would not have flourished in the presence of a pitch clock. He worked deliberately, making the O's big bopping first baseman Eddie Murray flail at a slider. He threw a fastball that had Ken Singleton swinging days late. The innings rolled by.

"I'll tell you, these two clubs are playing a hard-nosed ballgame in Chicago this afternoon," said Jones. "You've got a couple of pitchers in Storm Davis and Britt Burns that just refuse to wilt or fold."

The White Sox might finally have had something going in the seventh. Greg Walker singled past a sprawling Ripken to lead off, chasing Davis, who ceded the mound to Tippy Martinez.

La Russa lifted Walker for a pinch runner, Mike Squires. Vance Law singled, moving Squires to second.

Jerry Dybzinski, the Sox's light-hitting shortstop, took the sign and attempted to bunt Squires to third, but his bunt was a lousy one, bouncing once, high but not too high, and nowhere near far enough up the line to draw the third baseman in. Catcher Rick Dempsey sprang up, fielded it cleanly, and fired to Todd Cruz standing with his right foot on third to force Squires. Vance Law now stood at second, with Dybzinski on first, one out, with Julio Cruz, the number-nine hitter, coming up.

Julio Cruz slapped a base hit to short left. Gary Roenicke came up throwing, delivering a strike to Todd Cruz, the third baseman, who was standing in the grass of the infield between third and the mound. As Vance Law approached third, his third-base coach threw up a stop sign. Vance Law slowed, rounded the bag, then paused. Todd Cruz peeked at him, then noticed that Dybzinski had wandered too far off second, almost halfway to third. Todd Cruz began to run Dybzinski back, eventually throwing to second baseman Rich Dauer. Vance Law broke for home.

Dauer threw hurriedly to Dempsey, a little in front of the plate, and when Law arrived a fraction of a second later he attempted to bowl Dempsey over—but the backstop dropped his left shoulder in the manner of a fullback and Law caromed off him, spun inelegantly toward the backstop, and fell to the ground. Dempsey held on to the ball, retiring the runner. He glared at Dybzinski, who was frozen at second.

"I tell you, I don't know what these guys are thinking about in Chicago," said Brooks Robinson. "La Russa can't believe it either," he added over a shot of the Sox skipper pacing in the dugout, fuming.

With two outs and men at first and second, Martinez balked on a pickoff attempt to first, moving the runners over, but then got Rudy Law to fly out to end the frame.

Burns jumped out of the dugout and jogged to the mound. Back to work.

★★★

After a groundout and a strikeout, Burns was in good shape in the top of the eighth, but then Ripken took him to a full count before earning a walk. Eddie Murray followed that with a single, putting runners at first and second, with Roenicke coming up.

Salomé Barojas, a young righty from Córdoba, Mexico, began warming in the White Sox bullpen.

With the count at 3–0, Burns came too far inside, hitting Roenicke with a "glancing blow off the backside," as Robinson had it. The bases were loaded, and for the first time that afternoon, the Orioles saw a man reach third base.

It's hard for those of us accustomed to baseball circa 2025 to imagine that any manager would look at the situation before Tony La Russa—bases loaded, a scoreless tie in the eighth inning of an elimination game, starter having gone deep into the game, the DH spot due up next—and opt to leave his guy in there. But after a conversation on the mound with Burns and Fisk, that's exactly what La Russa did.

"Boy, I tell ya, who you got better than Burns, huh?" concluded Jones, displaying a reasoning that the ensuing decades have buried beneath binders full of data. "He's *really* done a job for the White Sox today."

Ken Singleton had started at DH for Baltimore that afternoon, but he had been lifted for a pinch runner, Al Bumbry, in the seventh. Now Bumbry was being replaced by Dan Ford.

Ford fouled back the first pitch and looked at the second, a fastball on the inside part of the plate, to quickly put Burns ahead 0–2. On the third pitch, Ford popped up to the second baseman for the third out. Still no score.

The bottom of the eighth and the top of the ninth passed without much excitement, and then in the bottom of the ninth, Martinez, still pitching in relief of Davis, got two quick outs but let the next two batters reach. One stolen base later and the Sox had runners at second and third, two out in the bottom of the ninth, and a chance to tie up the series and reward Burns's Herculean effort.

The tension was awful, unassuaged even by the sight of a clown standing in the aisle behind home plate, resisting context. Red polka dots on a white jumpsuit, a big red nose.

Rudy Law struck out looking.

Out came Burns once again.

★★★

The sun came out briefly, just in time to shine on John Shelby as he struck out looking for the first out in the top of the tenth. That brought Baltimore right fielder Tito Landrum to the plate as the clouds returned.

Does it foreshadow too much if I tell you that Tito Landrum had, to that point in his career, hit a total of three home runs? That he'd never hit one in the postseason, and would wind up playing nine years in the majors, retiring in 1988 with a grand total of thirteen regular season homers?

Am I jumping too far ahead if I tell you that in 1984 Burns went 4–12, got sent to the bullpen, and had the worst year of his professional career? Or that he rebounded in 1985 to win eighteen games, cement his place in the rotation, and earn a handful of Cy Young votes? Does it further complicate things if you learn that 1985 would be his final season as a big-league pitcher? That in December he would be traded along with two minor leaguers to the Yankees for Joe Cowley and Ron Hassey, but that before playing a single inning in the Bronx the pain in his hips would prove debilitating, and that doctors would discover osteoarthritis, and suggest that if he ever pitched again he risked depriving himself the ability to walk?

"It never not hurts," Burns later told the *New York Times*. "It's just a question of how much."

Landrum watched Burns's first pitch go by.

"So you think it's easy to win a championship, huh?" said Jones in the broadcast booth.

Burns's next pitch was straight, over the heart of the plate. In the parlance: he hung it.

Landrum, a right-handed hitter, lashed at it, and the ball lifted into the flat, grey, gusty Chicago sky before ricocheting off the face of the second deck in left and falling to the bleachers below.

"Home run, Tito Landrum," said Jones, a hint of disbelief in his voice. "It just cut a hole in the wind." Landrum sprinted around the bases and was being warmly greeted in the Baltimore dugout by the time Tony La Russa emerged from the Chicago bench to stride across the infield and take the ball from Burns.

As Burns made the lonely walk off the mound toward the White Sox clubhouse, the Baltimore players moved to the top step of the dugout and began applauding the Chicago starter. Rick Dempsey tipped his cap. The Orioles stood and heralded Burns, likely sensing the imminence of a result that would not fully reflect the quality of the work the Chicago starter had done that afternoon. Sometimes it takes the eye of an insider to fully appreciate these things.

★★★

Salomé Barojas came in to calm things down, but Cal Ripken Jr. slapped one up the middle and off Barojas's foot, for a single, and then Eddie Murray rapped a base hit to right. White Sox fans, does it hurt less in the retelling now that we know both hitters went on to be Hall of Famers? I'm guessing not.

Gary Roenicke singled to score Ripken. Altobelli sent John Lowenstein, a lefty, out to the on-deck circle to bat for Dan Ford in the DH spot. La Russa countered with Juan Agosto for a lefty-lefty matchup, which prompted Altobelli to call Lowenstein back to the bench in favour of Benny Ayala, a righty, and the fifth man to occupy the designated hitter's spot for the Orioles that day. Chess, American League–style.

Ayala lofted a ball into centre that backed Rudy Law up to the warning track. The wind whipped above the low-slung roof of intimate Comiskey Park, jerking the ball this way and that. Rudy Law danced, lurched, and finally dove forward, only barely managing the catch. Murray, waiting patiently on third, then trotted home. Checkmate.

Agosto was lifted for Dennis Lamp, who induced a ground ball to short from Dauer. The long half inning was over.

Tippy Martinez came back out to pitch the bottom of the tenth, now with a three-run lead. The air had gone out of the Chicago crowd. Even the clown had wandered away.

Fisk flied out to deep left. Baines singled, and stubborn hope kindled in the assembled hearts of the Chicago faithful. But

Luzinski struck out looking at a curveball that caught the outer half, and then Paciorek waved feebly over a breaking ball that bounced in front of Dempsey, who blocked it, cartwheeled awkwardly forward to retrieve it, and fired to Murray at first to record the final out.

That same night at Veterans Stadium, that enormous tub-shaped ark afloat in a sea of asphalt in south Philadelphia, the Phillies would ride a strong start from Steve Carlton and a three-run homer by Gary Matthews for a 7–2 victory over the Dodgers and a 3–1 series win to claim the National League pennant, earning the right to contest the Orioles for the World Series.

Back in Chicago, Comiskey Park, its tenants' schedule all done for the year, would be winterized, while the White Sox players prepared themselves for their long furlough.

★★★

In the years after his hip ailment forced him from baseball, Britt Burns wandered away from the game. He did a lot of elk hunting out west, did some hiking, and operated a ranch in Colorado. After a few years he thought he heard the game calling him back. Figuring he'd worked himself into good shape, he gave pitching another shot, auditioning for the Yankees in 1990 and the Red Sox in 1991. Neither attempt resulted in a big-league roster spot, but Burns discovered a fondness and knack for tutoring younger pitchers. He worked some of his old connections and wound up in the Marlins' organization, the pitching coach of their Rookie League team. Several years later he was named a coach of the Tigers' Triple A team in Toledo. Jobs with the Astros and White Sox organizations followed. Clearly,

Britt Burns had a place in the fraternity of professional baseball.

"A valiant effort from Britt Burns," Chuck Jones had said that afternoon at Comiskey. His peers had recognized it, even if the final score hadn't. It was no pennant, but you can't overstate the value of earning the respect of your fellow workers.

JOB RETRAINING

On diversifying one's skill set to extend a career

The last image most of us have of Brett Phillips is him wearing the bland, corporate blue-and-white Tampa Bay Rays uniform, the business card–font *T* and *B* interlocked on his shiny batting helmet. The lefty slashed a base hit to right-centre, and in the next moment Phillips was gleefully playing airplane, his arms spread wide as he ran around the outfield turf of Globe Life Field in Arlington, Texas, pursued by exuberant teammates.

It was Game Four of the 2020 World Series—a strange World Series that capped a sixty-game regular season, when games were played in empty stadiums before seats filled with cardboard cut-outs. The Rays, trailing the Dodgers by a run in the last of the ninth, sent Phillips to the plate with two runners on. Phillips slapped Kenley Jansen's 1–2 cutter for a base hit. Kevin Kiermaier rounded third and chugged home easily to tie the game. The trailing runner, Randy Arozarena, was seemingly caught out in no man's land midway up the third baseline. But a series of blunders by the Dodgers gave him life, so he dove headfirst toward home, coming to an abrupt rest in a Superman pose, his hands atop the plate, safe, having just scored the winning run. He smiled and began slapping the plate with his right hand, still lying on the ground. When Arozarena scored the run,

Phillips, cruising into second base, lost his mind, a jovial-seeming guy in a business-casual haircut whooping and wheeling across the expansive showroom floor, looking like he'd just set a new monthly sales record, pointing upward, drawing attention to the workings of heaven or, possibly, the stadium's shiny new roof.

That was pretty much the high point for fourth outfielder Brett Phillips. He'd just collected a game-winning hit to tie the World Series, but he wouldn't play at all in Game Five, and appeared only as a pinch-runner in Game Six—both of which LA won to claim the Series.

The following season, he was deployed more regularly by Rays manager Kevin Cash. Phillips played across the outfield, with some spot pinch-hitting and -running opportunities, and appeared in 118 games, improving his offensive numbers in the process.

In 2021, Phillips became that position player who eagerly jumps in to pitch in a blowout. He first did so in a game against the Blue Jays. He was loose and goofy in the bullpen as he tried out different deliveries, until he charged out from the bullpen to the mound. Once on the rubber, he served up fat eephus pitches that Toronto hitters smacked around, but everything stayed in the yard and the Rays managed to patch together three outs while giving up only one run.

Phillips continued to struggle with the bat in 2022 and played fewer games as a result. That might have imbued those spot-pitching assignments with more urgency; he was eager to find a new way to provide value to the team. He took the mound three times that season, soaking up innings in lost causes, easing the wear on essential bullpen parts. In each appearance he was giddy, lighthearted, whistling while he worked, singing while dangling off the edge of relevance.

The Rays designated him for assignment on August 1, then traded him to the Orioles, who played him a handful of times before parking him in the minors. He next appeared in the majors for the Angels for a brief spell the following September. Overall, he hit .175 for the Halos. After the season, he elected free agency.

The White Sox took a flier, inked him to a minor-league deal, and then shipped him to AAA Charlotte. The writing was on the wall: World Series heroics weren't going to guarantee him a spot on a major-league roster. That might have been the straw that broke the camel's back for Phillips—if he wasn't going to crack the lineup of the 2024 Chicago White Sox, a team that would eventually lose 121 games, then what lineup would he crack?

So Brett Phillips met up with Sean Gallagher, a retired pitcher who had pivoted to providing pitching instruction at a facility in suburban Austin, to reinvent himself. Brett Phillips was going to become a real pitcher.

There's a rich history of position players relocating to the mound. Generally, their profiles are similar to Phillips's: strong arm, weak bat. Statistics website baseball-reference.com lists 393 such players. You haven't heard of most of them, but then, any random sampling of professional baseball players will yield mostly unknowns.

A few you've probably heard of: Sean Doolittle was drafted as a first baseman and outfielder. Kenley Jansen, who gave up that RBI single to Phillips, was a catcher. Knuckleballer Tim Wakefield began his pro career as a first baseman. Hall of Fame starter Bob Lemon debuted at third base. Hall of Fame closer Trevor Hoffman started out as a shortstop. Those guys stand as ideals to someone like Phillips, their exploits providing enough in the way of motivation to push through another day of training, another day back near the bottom of professional baseball.

Phillips has some contemporaries too, other ex-position players trying to reinvent themselves. Alex Blandino converted from utility guy with a streaky bat into a knuckleballer, and he showed enough promise that the Reds offered him a contract. He was rattling around in the low minors the last I checked. And outfielder Anthony Gose played five years for the Blue Jays and Tigers before his conversion; he undertook a five-year climb back to the majors that culminated in a spot in the Guardians' bullpen.

But if Phillips was going to make something of his reset, his pitching couldn't look like the pitching he'd done in those blowout games. No lazy cement mixers, no slow, hanging curves.

In enlisting Gallagher's services, Phillips was doing the work necessary to successfully make the switch. According to Gallagher's website, the coach's "overall style and philosophy [is] geared around adaptation, progression and the forward-thinking methodology around all concepts of pitching and baseball." That's mealy-mouthed corporate garble, but you get the gist: he's going to make you hustle.

The rebuild showed early signs of progress. Phillips tested his stuff against college hitters in a summer league, topping out at 95 mph on the gun and with big drop on his curve. He had a slider and a changeup. You can imagine him thinking, "This might actually work!"

He joined the GPS Legends, a semipro team out of Texas, and headed to the 2024 National Baseball Congress World Series in Wichita. In his first appearance, he struck out the side in the first inning. His fastball hit 97 mph.

The Yankees were impressed and signed him to a minor-league deal. His first appearance didn't go well—he gave up five runs without recording an out. There was more work to do.

Not that the work guarantees any results. Sometimes effort's only end is more effort. And for most players who attempt this sort of career renovation, the road doesn't end in the Hall of Fame. Instead, it means you've managed to last a few more years in baseball. In *Bull Durham*, when manager Joe Riggins tells Crash Davis that he's been sent down several minor-league rungs so he can mentor a hotshot new pitcher, Davis asks what's in it for him. Says Riggins, "You can keep going to the ballpark and keep getting paid to do it."

Phillips wanted to keep getting paid to go to the ballpark. When market forces and desire ferment into desperation, crazy things can happen. A light-hitting utility guy just might find himself lighting up radar guns.

"The whole reason I'm doing this is I feel like I can still compete," said Phillips, explaining his motivation to the *Tampa Bay Times*. "I love the game. And I want to continue to play the game, especially at the highest level." There's also a very stark question for guys like Phillips and Blandino and Gose, who've spent their lives training and playing and climbing the levels of baseball only to stall or fall back, and who suddenly find their most marketable skill in scant demand: What else should they do?

To avoid answering that, they start training to develop new skills in the hopes of staying in the industry they love. Like Riggins tells Crash, "Beats the hell out of working at Sears." Because as dramatic a change as it might be to move from the grass to the mound, I have to believe it pales in comparison to making the jump to civilian life.

SHUCKS, MD

On inflated numbers, sticking around only as long as necessary, and true callings

A moment here to appreciate the mutability of memory: The records are complete enough to tease out a precise account of Hub Pruett's success against Babe Ruth. Over fifteen matchups in 1922, Pruett struck out Ruth nine times, walked him three, and allowed him only two hits—including a home run. Ruth struck out eighty times that season, meaning Pruett accounts for 11 percent of the total, which is so impressive you'd think no mythologizing would be necessary.

But in what amounts to a baseball fish story, or a game of statistical telephone, those numbers have morphed, grown, been embellished over the decades.

"Pruett, you may recall," said Hank Severeid in 1945, "fanned Ruth sixteen of the eighteen times he pitched to him during that [1922] season." This, mind you, from the man who caught the balls that Ruth missed.

In 1949, *The Sporting News* authoritatively claimed that Pruett "fanned Ruth the first thirteen times he faced him." That same year, the very same outlet revised the claim to "nine times in eleven tries." By 1957, their strikeout count was "ten times in thirteen official times at bat" in Hub's first season.

A decade after his retirement, Shucks, possibly having internalized the press's lionization of his exploits, declared, "I struck out New York's big Babe Ruth the first thirteen times I faced him."

I don't mean to ridicule the claimants, nor to diminish the accomplishment—there's no need to garnish the real numbers. For two seasons, Pruett dominated Ruth. I'm interested in the contrast between the ease with which we're now able to pore over historical documentation while seated comfortably in our homes and the difficulty of knowing in the past, when the numbers were printed on physical media but largely uncompiled and often incomplete. Even as trusted a publication as *The Sporting News* couldn't keep them straight. This is why researchers dig into the historical record, grounding in fact what's been burnished by our desire for myth.

But more than that, I'm struck by the flattening effect these numbers can have, even in a game as dependent on numbers as baseball. It's easy to call up Shucks's numbers on baseball-reference.com and marvel at his mastery of Ruth. But as Pruett's story so ably demonstrates, because the numbers fail to capture everything, they sure aren't up to the task of capturing a life.

★★★

You can't trace the fortunes of the St. Louis Browns without charting the career of George Sisler, and you can neatly cleave Sisler's career in two roughly equal halves. The pivot point is the winter between the 1922 and 1923 seasons. In the first half, Sisler is among the two or three best hitters in baseball. He plays eight seasons for the Browns and is a dazzling hitter, amassing a .361 average and recording two seasons of better than .400 (.407 in 1920, and .420 in 1922). In the latter half, Sisler is good—above average, certainly—but noticeably diminished. He is a .320 hitter across seven seasons—four more with the Browns followed by stints in Washington and Boston (NL) before he spent a couple of seasons wandering the minors and then calling it a day.

In the middle, sometime after St. Louis narrowly lost the AL pennant to the Yankees, and before the team was to report for spring training, Sisler caught the flu. Over the course of that illness, he developed a severe sinus infection, which in turn caused a "muscular disturbance" in his eye. He attested that he had "a case of double vision," which prevented him from playing a single game in 1923. He eventually returned to the Browns in '24; while still quite good, he was never the same ballplayer.

The Browns were sunk without their greatest offensive contributor. The 1923 season began with a pair of losses to Cobb and the Tigers at Sportsman's Park. Pruett started the second game and was roughed up, surrendering seven runs (six earned) and taking the loss. He pitched in relief twice over the next few days, and started again in Detroit, giving up five runs and taking his second loss. After four appearances, Shucks was 0–2 with an ERA of 6.19.

His chronically sore arm was still sore. The winter had done little to heal it, and no sooner had the season started when Lee Fohl began to lean heavily on his crafty second-year left-hander, tasked with starting or finishing games depending on circumstances, and rarely given more than a day or two between outings.

Much of the workload was likely the result of Fohl's awareness of Hub's success against the Babe. Pruett got his first shot at Ruth at home on May 16. Fohl inserted Hub in relief of Vangilder in the eighth, down 4–1. Hub walked Joe Dugan. Babe followed Dugan in the order.

Shucks sat him down on three pitches.

"I suppose one of the reasons I was so successful against Ruth is that I wasn't a rabid fan as a kid," Shucks later told *The Sporting News*. "Big baseball names didn't mean as much to me as they do to many other boys."

Shucks faced Ruth thirteen times in 1923. Ruth didn't fare much better than he had the year before, eking out a sacrifice and four walks, a pair of hits including a homer; he struck out five times.

But overall, Hub had come back down to earth. He would finish the season with a 4–7 record, an ERA that ballooned to 4.31, and considerable discomfort in his left arm. His inning total was down to 104. Without Sisler, and with a few other players backsliding, the Browns sunk to the bottom half of the standings.

★★★

Worsening arm trouble limited Pruett to just sixty-five innings in 1924, and he only faced Ruth five times, giving up three hits. Hub returned to the Browns for 1925, but his arm woes continued. The team optioned him to Oakland of the Pacific Coast League. His peregrinations had begun.

He threw 209 innings for the Oaks in 1925. He threw another 277 in 1926—more than twice as many as he'd ever thrown for the Browns.

In truth, Pruett was working with broken machinery. "I was a sore-armed pitcher from the day I broke into Organized

Baseball," he confessed to *The Sporting News*. "I broke three ribs pitching for Missouri University in my last year of college ball and I was never again able to throw freely."

Ahead of the 1927 season, Hub latched on with the Phillies, appearing in 31 games and going 7–17 for a team that lost 103 games. The Phillies put him on their reserved list for 1928 and he provided them with steady work through most of the summer, until the club sold him to the Newark Bears of the International League. The Bears leaned on him heavily down the stretch and brought him back for 1929. All the while, Pruett kept up his medical studies, taking classes at whichever institution was closest to wherever he happened to be playing ball.

This, it seems to me, is the more interesting version of Hubert Pruett's story: playing professional baseball as a summer job. It's hard for most of us to imagine being good enough to persist at one of the hardest things in the world, let alone to have such a casual relationship to it. I'll grant that Shucks was no superstar—except perhaps when he was facing Ruth—but he was good enough to hang around professional baseball for a decade while putting away money for school, even as he suffered physically the whole time. He laid his body on the line in order to learn how to mend others' bodies—talk about a calling.

At the end of the 1929 season, none other than John McGraw purchased Hub's contract from Newark with the aim of slotting him into the Giants rotation. Pruett worked 135.2 innings with middling results; this failed to impress McGraw. "Hub, you'd make one of the greatest pitchers in the business if you'd keep your mind on baseball instead of on medicine," said Muggsy, according to Maurice O. Shevlin of the *St. Louis Globe-Democrat*.

During spring training in 1931, Hub's mind wandered too far from the game for Muggsy's liking. *The Sporting News* declared that the skipper was "not paying much attention to Pruett, who has asked permission to continue his hospital work until late in May." The Giants held on to him until the end of June, then shipped him back to Newark.

Hub had made no secret of his plan to retire once he began to practise medicine, and he was nearing the end of his studies. Baseball had just about done everything he'd needed it to. He got one more trip to the majors when the National League's hard-luck Boston club picked him up for the 1932 season. He appeared in eighteen games, starting seven of them, but by the end of the year Boston's manager, Bill McKechnie, was echoing McGraw, telling Shucks that he ought to concentrate on medicine. "Your patients need you," he said, "and my patience is gone."

Hub graduated from St. Louis University as a Doctor of Medicine on June 7, 1932. It had taken thirteen years of schooling and twelve seasons of pro ball to get him there. He'd studied at St. Louis University, the University of Chicago, Washington University in St. Louis, the University of Tennessee, and Rush University, and he always returned to SLU to write his exams and to intern.

He never made it back to the American League after leaving the Browns, so he never had another chance to face Ruth on a ball field. Pruett's final professional record, across all levels, was 92 wins against 103 losses. He'd racked up 1,791 innings of work. He took the state medical exam in January 1933, and then Dr. Hubert Shelby Pruett slipped away from baseball as easily as he'd slid into it, moving instead into a lifetime of medical service.

***

While still with the Browns, Hub had married Elsie Borgmann, and the couple had lived with her parents in a house on Sullivan Avenue in St. Louis, about a block east of Sportsman's Park. Their first daughter, Mary Jane, arrived in short order.

After his retirement from baseball, Hub set up his medical practice on St. Louis Avenue near Grand, just south of the ballpark. He and Elsie would eventually have two daughters and two sons, raising them in a house in Ladue, a suburb west of downtown St. Louis.

In June 1948, Shucks saw Ruth again. It was the first time they'd spoken, the first time they'd met outside of the simple binary arrangement of a mound and a plate. The occasion, reported by *The Sporting News*, was a luncheon in St. Louis in Ruth's honour. Ruth was quite ill; in a month he'd be dead.

Hub thanked the Babe for putting him through medical school. "If it hadn't been for you," he told the slugger, "I would have been a baseball unknown. Whatever fame I had was due to you."

"If all pitchers were like you," replied Ruth, "no one would have heard of me."

Shucks went on to sponsor Little League teams and play in Old-Timers games. He did repairs around the house, injuring his back in 1958 after falling while trying to fix a downspout. He watched his sons play football, and he played in dads-versus-dads baseball games at John Burroughs Preparatory School with his old teammate George Sisler. He wrote a book called *Baseball Hygienics*. He collected jazz records.

He treated Dizzy Dean's sore pitching arm and patched up Lefty Leifield when he returned from a quail-hunting trip with some pellets in his leg. Leifield had pitched for the Browns a few years before Hub, then turned to coaching. He'd helped the young Pruett with his curveball. When Lefty asked what he owed for the medical services, Shucks waved him off.

Pruett received one Hall of Fame vote every year from 1949 to 1953, and another in 1975. His name surfaced from time to time in the baseball press as a curio, a fun fact, for a where-are-they-now piece. The doctor who struck out Babe Ruth. It seems likely that his unusual story popped into the heads of *The Sporting News* writers as they encountered him around town, especially at the St. Louis Athletic Club, where he served as the in-house physician. There are times of the year when baseball stories are few and far between, and Shucks was always right there.

Elsie died in 1972. Hub continued to practise medicine, putting in forty-one years once all was said and done. He lived almost fifty years after he'd thrown his last big-league pitch. The last typed entry on his yellowed index card, stored for decades alongside 180,000 other player entries in an office in downtown St. Louis, reads: "Died in Ladue, Missouri, January 28, 1982."

When Shucks was a young man, a scout got a look at him and liked what he saw, and so Pruett was offered a unique opportunity. But Shucks wasn't interested in the usual arrangement, the total commitment required to make it as a ballplayer, followed by the desperate action needed to cling to a roster spot for as long as possible. Instead, he rearranged the relationship between work and play, using the game to fund the pursuit of his lifelong career. Though unconventional, the transaction worked out well: The Browns got two years of a lefty who could strike out Babe Ruth seemingly at will. The people of St. Louis got a medical professional dedicated to their well-being.

And Hubert Shelby Pruett got to live a full and varied life on his own terms.

Not that I believe Pruett intentionally disrupted an established model. I'm sure his thinking was more immediate than that, and ran along the lines of using what he had to get what he wanted. From our vantage, his story is unique for its details. But more broadly, it holds a shape common to the lives most of us live in our systems of trade and debt, compensation and value. We try to balance our needs and our wants. Try to figure out how to leverage what fate gives us and what reality requires when we get out of bed in the morning. And in the margins and crevices, those spaces left unsullied by commerce, we do what we can to eke out a little room for the parts of ourselves that can't be accounted for in a ledger.

SOURCES

A list—almost certainly incomplete—of sources consulted during the writing of this book

Digital resources

Andrew Clem's Baseball: Our National Pastime and Its "Green Cathedrals" (andrewclem.com/Baseball/index.html)

Ballpark Digest (ballparkdigest.com)

Baseball Digest archives (baseballdigest.com)

Baseball Reference (baseball-reference.com)

New York Times archives (nytimes.com)

Retrosheet (retrosheet.org)

The Society for American Baseball Research (SABR.org)

The Sporting News archive (paperofrecord.hypernet.ca/search_paper.asp?PaperId=834)

The Sporting News Baseball Player Contract Cards Collection (digital.la84.org/digital/collection/p17103coll3)

Sports Illustrated archives (si.com)

I also made extensive use of general public internet sources such as YouTube, newspapers.com, and MLB.com.

Film and video

The Pruitt-Igoe Myth: An Urban History, directed by Chad Freidrichs, 2011.

The Saint of Second Chances, directed by Jeff Malmberg and Morgan Neville, 2023.

The St. Louis Browns: The Team That Baseball Forgot, directed by Justin Tolliver, 2018.

Books

Edward Achorn, *Fifty-nine in '84: Old Hoss Radbourn, Barehanded Baseball, and the Greatest Season a Pitcher Ever Had*, Harper, 2011.

Jeremy Beer, *Oscar Charleston: The Life and Legend of Baseball's Greatest Forgotten Player*, University of Nebraska Press, 2019.

Bill Borst, Bill Rogers, and Ed Wheatley, *St. Louis Browns: The Story of a Beloved Team*, Reedy Press, 2017.

Frank Deford, *The Old Ball Game: How John McGraw, Christy Mathewson, and the New York Giants Created Modern Baseball*, Grove Atlantic, 2002.

Peter Dreier and Robert Elias, *Baseball Rebels: The Players, People, and Social Movements That Shook Up the Game and Changed America*, University of Nebraska Press, 2022.

Curt Flood with Richard Carter, *The Way It Is*, Trident, 1971.

Thomas W. Gilbert, *How Baseball Happened: Outrageous Lies Exposed! The True Story Revealed*, David R. Gordine, 2020.

Bill James, *The New Bill James Historical Baseball Abstract*, Free Press, 2001.

Martin Donell Kohout, *Hal Chase: The Defiant Life and Turbulent Times of Baseball's Biggest Crook*, McFarland, 2001.

Bernard Malamud, *The Natural*, Harcourt, Brace & Company, 1952.

David Nemec, *The Beer and Whiskey League: The Illustrated History of the American Association—Baseball's Renegade Major League*, The Lyons Press, 2004.

Richard Peterson, ed., *The St. Louis Baseball Reader*, University of Missouri Press, 2006.

Lawrence S. Ritter, *The Glory of Their Times: The Story of the Early Days of Baseball Told by the Men Who Played It*, Vintage, 1985.

Ron Shelton, *The Church of Baseball: The Making of* Bull Durham, Knopf, 2022.

Brad Snyder, *A Well-Paid Slave: Curt Flood's Fight for Free Agency in Professional Sports*, Penguin, 2007.

Steve Steinberg, *Urban Shocker: Silent Hero of Baseball's Golden Age*, University of Nebraska Press, 2017.

Bill Veeck with Ed Linn, *Veeck as in Wreck: The Autobiography of Bill Veeck*, University of Chicago Press, 2001.

Lonnie Wheeler, *The Bona Fide Legend of Cool Papa Bell: Speed, Grace, and the Negro Leagues*, Abrams, 2021.

ACKNOWLEDGEMENTS

Thanks are due to Amelie Mancini, the artist whose postcard collection, Curious Second Careers, featuring baseball players with odd jobs, planted the seed many years ago that would one day grow into this book. The first sentence of "Workingman's Blues" is taken directly from her work, and is used here with permission.

I owe an enormous debt of gratitude to the researchers of the Society for American Baseball Research (SABR.org), dozens if not hundreds of whom contributed to scholarship that went into the writing of this book. Quite simply, this work would not be possible without their quiet, dogged efforts. If you read and enjoyed this book, I encourage you to become a member, if you have not already done so.

Thanks to Jamie Pruett and the family of Hubert Shelby Pruett for sharing his story with me. I hope I've done Hub's remarkable life some justice.

Thanks to James Mahoney and Richard Puerzer, as well as my editor, Andrew Faulkner, for their work fact-checking this book. If any errors remain the fault is entirely mine. Their efforts were nothing short of heroic.

To the Assembly team—Leigh, Debby, and Andrew—thank you. A new home that feels like an old home. I'm humbled by and grateful for the work you do.

And to Andrew: you're 3-for-3. That's a heck of a good game. Thanks once again.

Thanks to the players, coaches, and parents of the Peterborough Tigers 2010 teams that I had the great privilege of watching, cheering, and coaching. Remember to tag up, boys.

Thanks to J. Daniel, Tom Gilbert, Bill Humber, Sandra Marchetti, Lewis MacLeod, Norm Nehmetallah, and Rob Winger for support, encouragement, and answers to a variety of questions during the writing of this book.

Thanks to my dad, Gord Forbes, for a love of the game, for company at Blue Jays games, and on long GO Train rides to and from Union Station.

Thanks to Adelaide, Cormac, and Theo for being a part of so many of the memories contained herein, and for teaching me how to be a father.

This book is for Christie, as always. It is dedicated to the memory of Kevin Curley, and to the memory of my mother, Mary Uldene MacKinnon.

PHOTO CREDIT: ALICE WINCHESTER

ANDREW FORBES is the author of two previous collections of baseball writing, *The Utility of Boredom* (2016) and *The Only Way Is the Steady Way* (2021), as well as two short story collections, a novel, and a novella. He has been shortlisted for the Danuta Gleed Literary Award, and named a finalist for the Trillium Book Award. His work has appeared in publications such as the *Toronto Star*, *Canadian Notes & Queries*, and *Maisonneuve* magazine. Born in Ottawa, Forbes has lived in Atlantic Canada and rural Eastern Ontario, and now resides in Peterborough, Ontario.

RECYCLED
Paper
FSC® C100212

Printed by Imprimerie Gauvin
Gatineau, Québec